D1090672

ALL THE PLANTS OF THE BIBLE

Pomegranate and Fig
And Saul tarried . . . under a pomegranate tree . . . I SAMUEL 14:2
Whoso keepeth the fig tree shall eat the fruit thereof . . . PROVERBS 27:18

ALL THE PLANTS OF THE BIBLE

TEXT AND ILLUSTRATIONS BY

Winifred Walker

DOUBLEDAY & COMPANY, INC.
GARDEN CITY, NEW YORK
1979

ISBN: 0-385-14964-6
Library of Congress Catalog Card Number 78-22802

Copyright © 1957 by Winifred Walker
All rights reserved.

Design by M Franklin–Plympton

PRINTED IN THE UNITED STATES OF AMERICA

Contents

Frontispiece: POMEGRANATE AND FIG

The illustration for each plant appears opposite the text.

(5)

Supplement I   219

Supplement II   236

(6)

Preface

From earliest childhood I had been swayed by the rhythm of the words from the Scriptures. What, I wondered, were the costly frankincense and myrrh borne by the Wise Men from the East on their pilgrimage to the Babe at Bethlehem? Where were these plants grown?

For years I was unable to find satisfying botanical answers to my questions. When my vocation as a trained artist was established, I was asked to make faithful watercolor portraits of flowers not native to the Western Hemisphere but grown here from seed brought back by those hardy adventurers of the past who had discovered them in India. The pictures of these beautiful flowers were housed in the archives of The Horticultural Society in Westminster. However, I was still to receive the inspiration to create paintings of the Bible flora. A year later I arrived in the United States to accept the appointment of artist in the Department of Animal Husbandry at Davis, a branch of the University of California in Berkeley. Finally, I read a descriptive list issued by the New York Botanical Garden that gave over one hundred and fifty names of trees, herbs, and flowers of the Bible, along with their generic names and scriptural verses. It had been compiled by one of their curators, Dr. Harold N. Moldenke, who was responsible for the background research on which they based their famous "Bible Plant" exhibit. Now at last I knew that the frankincense tree grows in the Himalayas, and the myrrh, which exudes its gum for purifying, lives in the fierce heat of Yemen in Arabia. Also, I learned that the spikenard was from the valleys of Tibet and I determined to locate every plant mentioned on the list. Five years of this research made it possible for me to paint the illustrations for this book. All are from life except the balm, bdellium, spikenard, and frankincense, which perforce had to be portrayed from pressed specimens loaned to me by the University of California herbariums at Berkeley and Westwood.

Winifred Walker

(7)

Algum Tree

---

*And Solomon sent to Huram the king of Tyre,
saying, . . . Behold, I build an house to the
name of the Lord my God, to dedicate it to him.
. . . Send me now therefore a man cunning to
work in gold, and in silver. . . . Send me also
cedar trees, fir trees, and algum trees, out of Lebanon: for I know that thy servants can skill to
cut timber in Lebanon . . . Even to prepare me
timber in abundance.*

II CHRONICLES 2:3, 4, 7, 8, 9

This tree known to King Solomon as "algum" was the lofty *Juniperus excelsa,* or Grecian juniper, regarded also as a savin. It reaches a height of sixty-five feet and grows in the shape of a pyramid. The branches are spreading, and covered with finely cut heavy foliage. Flowers are borne in the shape of nodding catkins, and the fruit that follows is black and globular, joined close to the branches. This tree is abundant in the woods covering the mountains of Lebanon and Gilead, and was eminently suitable for the temple King Solomon was building for the Lord God; *"for the house which I am about to build shall be wonderful great."* II CHRONICLES 2:9. He must have regarded the wood of sufficient value to be brought from a country as far distant as Ophir. King Solomon's ships, the ships of Tarshish, were sent thither from Ezion-Geber, a port on the Red Sea. Voyages were made once in every three years, the ships returning to Israel freighted with gold, spices, ivory, algumwood, and ebony.

Algum Tree Juniperus excelsa   Hebrew: algummin
Send me also cedar trees, fir trees, and algum trees . . .
II CHRONICLES 2:8

Almond

And the Lord spake unto Moses, saying, Speak unto the children of Israel, and take of every one of them a rod . . . write thou every man's name upon his rod. And thou shalt write Aaron's name upon the rod of Levi. . . . And it came to pass, that on the morrow Moses went into the tabernacle of witness; and, behold, the rod of Aaron . . . was budded, and brought forth buds, and bloomed blossoms, and yielded almonds. NUMBERS 17:1, 2, 3, 8

The almond tree blooms in Israel as early as January, its flowers appearing long before the leaves. Blossoms are pink and sometimes white, and the tree in bloom has been likened to a hoary-headed patriarch. It belongs to the peach family, and its fruit is wrapped in a heavy covering, wrinkled and leathery, that encases the shell of the nut. The kernels are narrow and orange, becoming a rich creamy white when peeled. These are used universally to produce oil. One hundred and fourteen pounds of fruit will yield fifty pounds of oil. Apparently the almond was not grown in Egypt, for when famine was sore in the land, Jacob commanded his sons to journey there to ask help of the governor, who was his own son Joseph. "*. . . carry down the man a present, a little balm, and a little honey, spices, and myrrh, nuts, and almonds . . .*" GENESIS 43:11. Many wild almonds on Mount Carmel grow to a height of sixteen feet. Throughout the Era of the Maccabees the almond was the design on the shekel.

Almond Amygdalus communis   Hebrew: shaked

. . . I see a rod of an almond tree JEREMIAH 1:11

Almug Tree

---

*And the navy also of Hiram, that brought gold
from Ophir, brought in from Ophir great plenty
of almug trees, and precious stones. And the
king made of the almug trees pillars for the house
of the Lord, and for the king's house, harps also
and psalteries for singers: there came no such
almug trees, nor were seen unto this day.*

I KINGS 10:11, 12

The almug tree provided the sweet-scented timber for the temple
that Solomon built. It is native to southern India where it is
known either as red sandalwood or "red sanders wood," and
grows to the size of a walnut tree, about twenty feet high. The
trunk is four feet in circumference, and so strong and antiseptic is
the wood that no insects can live in it. Blossoms are pea-like, and
the fruit forms pods. The timber is very heavy and fine-grained,
black outside and inside a rich ruby red. It will take a fine polish,
and its scent must have made it pleasant to use. As the biblical text
indicates, musical instruments, harps, and psalteries were made
from the almug. The psaltry was a harp, lighter than that of
today, and known as *kinnor*. Almug wood contains tannin; when
mixed with sapan, it makes a good dye that gives a rich, red tone
to silks and wools. Sandalwood was also strewn upon couches and
used to perfume dwelling houses.

Almug Tree Pterocarpus santalinus   Hebrew: almuggim

. . . brought in from Ophir great plenty of almug trees . . .

I KINGS 10:11

Aloes (N.T.)

And after this Joseph of Arimathaea, being a dis-
ciple of Jesus, . . . besought Pilate that he might
take away the body of Jesus. . . . And there
came also Nicodemus, which at the first came to
Jesus by night, and brought a mixture of myrrh
and aloes, about an hundred pound weight.
Then took they the body of Jesus, and wound it
in linen clothes with the spices, as the manner of
the Jews is to bury.   JOHN 19:38, 39, 40

This is the true aloe, native to the island of Socotra in the Indian Ocean at the entrance to the Gulf of Aden. It is a handsome succulent plant, with thick fleshy leaves forming a heavy rosette just above the root. From this cluster rises the tall, leafless stem of the flower that belongs to the lily family. The spike-shaped inflorescence, made up of many bell-shaped flowers each nearly two inches long, is bright vermilion shading to clear yellow with a maize pistil. Its blue-gray leaves contain aloin, a substance which could be dissolved in water and added to sweet-smelling incenses for purifying the bodies of the departed. The condensed juice of the aloe is a strong purgative, well known to the ancients, and used by the Egyptians and the Greeks. The liquid when pressed from the leaves is bright violet.

Aloes (N.T.) Aloe succotrina   Greek: aloē

. . . and brought a mixture of myrrh and aloes . . . JOHN 19:39

Aloes (O.T.)

As the valleys are they spread forth, as gardens
by the river's side, as the trees of lign aloes
which the Lord hath planted. . . .

NUMBERS 24:6

. . . thy God, hath anointed thee with the oil
of gladness above thy fellows. All thy garments
smell of myrrh, and aloes, . . . out of the ivory
palaces. . . .   PSALMS 45:7, 8

This is the lign aloe of the Old Testament. It is known as eagle-
wood, as its Latin name indicates, and is native to tropical Asia.
Agallochum is the heartwood of the tree. In form the tree is large
and spreading, and contains a dark-colored fragrant substance to
be found in its inner trunk or center. The branches of the
younger wood are white and almost scentless. In northern India it
attains the height of one hundred and twenty feet. So ancient is
the history of the lign aloe tree that it was noted by Herodotus
and other early writers as producing a substance of the greatest
value. In the East its wood, which takes a high polish and reveals a
lovely grain, was esteemed above all others. The soft and fragrant
inner wood was molded and used as a setting for precious stones.
To the ancients, it was worth its weight in gold. There is a popu-
lar belief in the East that this aloe is the only tree that has de-
scended to man from the Garden of Eden, all others being lost.
According to this legend, Adam brought away from the garden
one of its shoots, transplanted it in the land where he settled, and
all other aloes have sprung from this shoot. To this day it is called
Shoot of Paradise and Paradise Wood.

Aloes (O.T.) Aquilaria agallocha   Hebrew: ahâlim
All thy garments smell of myrrh, and aloes . . . PSALMS 45:8

Anise (dill)

---

*Woe unto you, scribes and Pharisees, hypocrites!
for ye pay tithe of mint and anise . . . and have
omitted the weightier matters of the law, judgment, mercy, and faith: these ought ye to have
done, and not to leave the other undone.*

MATTHEW 23:23

Thus Jesus had spoken to the multitude. He pointed out the will-
ful blindness of the Pharisees to their own shortcomings, giving as
example that they were outwardly clean and godly, but inwardly
guilty of extortion and excess. The plant here mentioned is the
dill, wrongly translated "anise," which in biblical days was rare in
Palestine. The Latinized Greek name *anethum* assures that it is
the dill. In growth it resembles fennel, and has flowerets of bright
golden yellow that form an umbel. It is a carminative and
yields essential oil. From ancient times, foods and essences have
been flavored with the plant, and it has been used medicinally and
as a healing wash for skin wounds. Pliny, the historian and natu-
ralist, records still other uses of dill. It grows three feet high; the
fine-cut leaves are of a clear green, with paler stalks. The oval
fruits are brown and hard, and have a pungent taste. Dill was
grown by the ancient Greeks and Romans. The Talmud records
that the seeds, stems, and leaves were subject to tithe. In India
today the dill fruit is used as a universal medicine. It is the *shabath*
of Tolama, and is known to the Arabs as *shibith*.

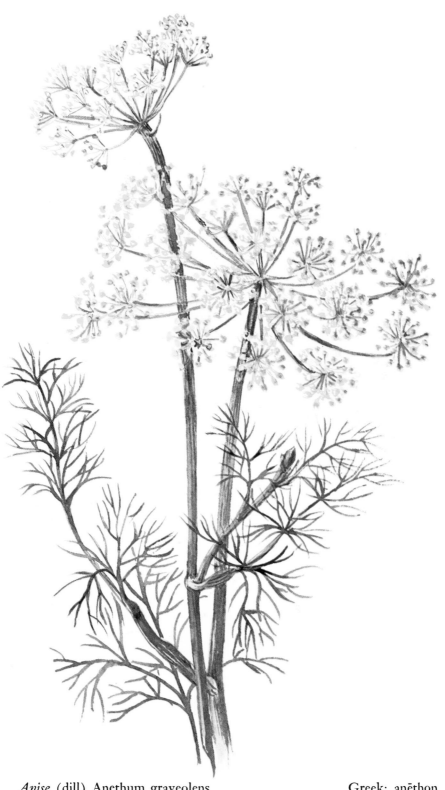

Anise (dill) Anethum graveolens Greek: anēthon
. . . *ye pay tithe of mint and anise and cummin* . . . MATTHEW 23:23

Apple (apricot)

A word fitly spoken is like apples of gold in pictures of silver.   PROVERBS 25:11

Thus spoke Solomon, son of David, the King of Israel, to his people. He exhorted them to teach wisdom and understanding that they too might receive equity, justice, and sound judgment. Young men must absorb knowledge and use discretion; wise men listen to counsel, and deliver sound speech at the right time. The "apples of gold" are now thought to have been apricots, a fruit abounding in the Holy Land. True apples were of very poor quality then and are unlikely to have been the "apples of gold." The apricot belongs to the plum family and was early introduced into Palestine from Armenia, as its botanical name implies. Apples grew wild in the Caucasus. In Africa the apricot is regarded second only to the peach. Nearly thirty feet in height, it blossoms early, bearing close to the branches pale rose flowers with rich carmine shading in the center. The leaf, heart-shaped and borne on a long stalk often of bright red, has an underside much paler than the top, hence catching the light when the wind causes it to quiver. Trunk, boughs, and the branches bearing the fruit are rough and gnarled. Prussic acid, long used in medicine, is produced from the kernels. The apricot has a strong, revitalizing perfume, as the words of Solomon indicate: "*Comfort me with apples for I am sick.*" It was cultivated in China two thousand years before the Christian Era, and is recorded by Pliny and Dioscorides. In the SONG OF SOLOMON 2:3 are these poetic words: "*As the apple tree among the trees of the wood, so is my beloved among the sons. I sat down under his shadow with great delight, and his fruit was sweet to my taste.*"

Apple (apricot) Prunus armeniaca   Hebrew: tappuach

   . . . like apples of gold in pictures of silver. PROVERBS 25:11

Balm (balsam)

*Judah, and the land of Israel, . . . they traded
in thy market wheat of Minnith, and pannag, and
honey, and oil, and balm.*   EZEKIEL 27:17

The fabulous city of Tyre had to listen to the chastising words
of the Lord God. The people were reminded of their great
wealth, accumulated in trading with other districts, and they
heard *"For thus saith the Lord God; . . . I will make thee a ter-
ror, and thou shalt be no more. . . .* EZEKIEL 26:19, 21. Balm or
balsam is the gum or thickened juice exuding from the balsam
tree that was very prolific in Judea. It is native to southern Arabia
and Ethiopia; at one time it was cultivated on the plains of
Jericho, so the Jews believed that it was planted there by King
Solomon. According to history, the first roots were brought to
him by the Queen of Sheba at the time she paid him her royal
visit. I KINGS 10:10 records: *"And she gave the king . . . of spices
very great store, and precious stones: there came no more such
abundance of spices as these which the queen of Sheba gave to
king Solomon."* So rare and so costly was the plant that it was
later exhibited in the streets of Rome for all the people to see. On
the first occasion it was brought by Pompey, after the first con-
quest of Judea. Again when Vespasian destroyed Jerusalem, the
balm tree was among the spoils. The balm was an emblem of Palestine, and shrubs in cultivation were protected by guards to keep
them safe. It is trained like a vine, has scanty foliage and flowers
like tufts of acacia blossoms. A reddish black and pulpy nut contains a seed that is fragrant and yellow. The plant is much used in
medicine.

Balm (balsam) Commiphora opobalsamum   Hebrew: tsori

. . . they traded in thy market . . . honey, and oil, and balm.

EZEKIEL 27:17

Balm

And they sat down to eat bread: and they lifted up their eyes and looked, and, behold, a company of Ishmeelites came from Gilead with their camels bearing spicery and balm and myrrh, going to carry it down to Egypt. GENESIS 37:25

The balm here recorded is the false balm of Gilead found in quantity on the plains surrounding the Dead Sea. This evergreen shrub grows twelve to fourteen feet high. Its leaves are a rich green and it bears a pretty white blossom that turns into a green applelike fruit, coloring later to a rich purple. These fruits are picked before they ripen, and from them a sweet oil is extracted. This modern balm, growing east of Jordan in the land of Gilead, is called *lukkum* by the Arabs and sold by them as balm of Gilead. The gum resin from the bark gives fragrance and value to the plant, and until the seventeenth century was the ingredient of many medicines. Unlike most resins, it soon softens with even moderate heat. An oil that is also extracted is prepared by the Arabs of Jericho and sold in large quantities to pilgrims. Jeremiah's exclamation *"Is there no balm in Gilead?"* has passed into a household saying; and the same prophet advises the daughter of Egypt to *"go up to Gilead and take balm."* Babylon also was advised to *"take balm for her pain, if so she may be healed."*

Balm Balanites aegyptiaca   Hebrew: tsori
Is there no balm in Gilead? . . . JEREMIAH 8:22

Barley

---

*So there was hail, and fire mingled with the hail,
very grievous. . . . And Pharaoh sent, and
called for Moses and Aaron, and said unto them,
I have sinned this time: the Lord is righteous, and
I and my people are wicked. And . . . the barley
was smitten: for the barley was in the ear. . . .*

EXODUS 9:24, 27, 31

This was part of the story of the plagues sent by the Lord God to punish Pharaoh for not allowing the children of Israel to leave Egypt. Barley is sown in Israel in the autumn, through the months of October and November. It is gathered in the spring, at the season of Passover. A second sowing is done when the winter is past. A bread was made from barley, and was a staple food of the Hebrews. As an article of diet, it has been cultivated for man and beast from remotest antiquity, and is a universally grown cereal today. Barley has a smaller protein content than wheat or rye, and was a symbol of poverty in a household. The Hebrew word *seorah* means "long hair," and here refers to the awns, which are very long. There are two kinds of barley, one producing six, the other two, rows of grain. It has been found in the Egyptian tombs in Thebes, and in the dwellings of the Stone Age. The artificers engaged in the construction of Solomon's Temple were given twenty thousand measures of barley as their food ration. In the New Testament, loaves made from barley were given to the multitudes by Jesus. ". . . *Andrew, Simon Peter's brother, saith unto him, There is a lad here, which hath five barley loaves, and two small fishes. . . . So the men sat down, in number about five thousand.*" JOHN 6:8, 9, 10.

Barley Hordeum distichon   Hebrew: seorah   Greek: krithe
A land of wheat, and barley . . . DEUTERONOMY 8:8
The above illustration shows both barley and rie. The heads of grain on
the right are the barley.

Bdellium

And the Lord God planted a garden eastward in Eden. . . . And out of the ground made the Lord God to grow every tree that is pleasant to the sight, and good for food; . . . there is bdellium and the onyx stone.   GENESIS 2:8, 9, 12

Parkinson, the sixteenth-century English herbalist, writes that the tree which provides the aromatic gum known as bdellium grew in Havilah, the territory eastward of Persia. He goes on to say that the leaves resemble those of an oak, and when the bark is incised, the gum that oozes out is "the bigness of a white olive." Pliny mentions it around the first century A.D. as an odoriferous gum from a tree growing in Arabia Felix. He also states that it was sent from Bactria in India. When the gum was removed from the bark of the tree, the pieces would soon harden. They became transparent and waxlike, and looked like pearl. The women of Egypt were wont to carry little pouches filled with these pieces of bdellium, for they have a delightful perfume. The bdellium appears again in Holy Writ, in the book of NUMBERS 11:6, 7: *"But now our soul is dried away: there is nothing at all, beside this manna, . . . and the colour thereof as the colour of bdellium."*

Bdellium Commiphora africana   Hebrew: bedolach

. . . there is bdellium and the onyx stone. GENESIS 2:12

Beans

---

*And it came to pass, when David was come to
Mahanaim, that Shobi the son of Nahash of
Rabbah . . . and Machir the son of Ammiel
. . . brought beds, and basons, and earthen vessels, and wheat, . . . and parched corn, and
beans, . . . for the people that were with him,
to eat: for they said, The people is hungry, and
weary, and thirsty, in the wilderness.*

II SAMUEL 17:27, 28, 29

So ancient is this vegetable that it is recorded by Pliny. The bean
grows as an annual. It attains a height of three feet, has thick and
angular stems, firm, grayish-green leaves with light undersides,
and scented blossoms that are pea-shaped, creamy white, and with
a black blotch on the upright petals. Today, beans are very
widely cultivated in Syria and Egypt and provide a staple article
of diet. Beans are sometimes mixed in with grain flour to make a
wholesome bread. Beans are fed to horses and the stalks are given
to camels. In December the fields are sown with these legumes,
the blossoms appearing the third week in February. At the end of
June, at the time of the wheat harvest, the crop is ripe and ready
to be gathered. In ancient days beans were used in collecting
votes from the people: a white bean signifying approval of the
measure proposed; a black one, condemnation. Magistrates were
elected by the casting of beans. However, the priests of Egypt
were averse to them, even to feeling defiled from handling them.

Beans Vicia faba   Hebrew: pol
. . . *flour, and parched corn, and beans* . . . II SAMUEL 17:28

Bitter Herbs

And the Lord spake unto Moses, saying, Speak unto the children of Israel, saying, . . . he shall keep the passover unto the Lord. The fourteenth day of the second month at even they shall keep it, and eat it with unleavened bread and bitter herbs. They shall leave none of it unto the morning, nor break any bone of it: according to all the ordinances of the passover they shall keep it.   NUMBERS 9:9, 10, 11, 12

The dandelion was one of the bitter herbs of the Old Testament. Others were endive, chicory, lettuce, and sorrel. These were gathered fresh and eaten as salad. The grand feast of the Passover continued seven days, the first and last days being the most solemn. A lamb was to be slain as sacrifice, and eaten in Jerusalem only. The offering was to be taken, roasted entirely, and consumed the same night along with bitter herbs and unleavened bread made of wheaten flour, that was ground daily in small stone mills and served in the form of thin cakes. Leavened bread, or the sourdough left from the previous day, was forbidden to the Hebrews during the seven days of the Passover, in memory of their ancestors who had to flee in haste from Egypt. The bitter herb, dandelion, is native to southern Europe and today grows in many lands. Its name derives from the French *dent de lion*, inspired by the pointed edges of the leaves which turn downward to resemble a lion's tooth. Both dandelion and chicory roots are ground and used as decoctions. Today in some countries they are added to coffee as adulterants.

Bitter Herbs Taraxacum officinale   Hebrew: merorim

. . . eat it with unleavened bread and bitter herbs. NUMBERS 9:11

Box Tree

. . . I am with thee: . . . for I am thy God. . . .
I will make the wilderness a pool of water, . . .
I will plant in the wilderness the cedar, the
shittah tree, . . . I will set in the desert the fir
tree, and the pine, and the box tree together:
That they may see, and know, and consider, and
understand together, that the hand of the Lord
hath done this. . . .   ISAIAH 41:10, 18, 19, 20

The box tree grows in Lebanon, and is referred to as a forest tree.
It is also found on the Galilean hills and inhabits the Mediterranean region, there reaching a height of fifteen to twenty feet.
The leaves, as the scientific name of the plant implies, are much
longer than those of the European box. Ovid writes of its contin-
ual verdancy. For centuries the wood has been used in making
musical instruments. It has also provided fine inlays for cabinet
work, and has been much prized by engravers. Spoons and combs
have been fashioned from it. The grain is fine, hard, and compact.
It was a favorite bush with the Roman masters of topiary work,
who clipped it into many forms for their ornamental gardens. In
England, many tombs dating from the Roman occupation have
been unearthed and found to contain sprigs of box, no doubt to
represent the myrtle used similarly in Italy. Box has black glossy
seeds that can be fatal to animals when eaten.

Box Tree Buxus longifolia   Hebrew: teasshur

. . . *the pine, and the box tree together* . . . ISAIAH 41:19

Bramble

The trees went forth on a time to anoint a king over them; and they said unto the olive tree, Reign thou over us. But the olive tree said unto them, Should I leave my fatness, wherewith by me they honour God and man, and go to be promoted over the trees? Then said all the trees unto the bramble, Come thou, and reign over us. And the bramble said unto the trees, If in truth ye anoint me king over you, then come and put your trust in my shadow. . . .

JUDGES 9:8, 9, 14, 15

Thus Jotham, by using a parable, rebuked the evil men of Shechem who had set up Abimelech as king. *Rubus* is the classical name of the bramble; the leaves of this species resemble those of the elm tree. Its Anglo-Saxon name is *bremel*. A powerful bush-like plant, it throws long and strong arching stems across large tracts of the countryside, often impeding the traveler. Plum-colored branches are covered with soft gray down, yet are armed with long broad-based prickles and thorns. Leaves of rich clear green, white-felted underneath, have edges cut into fine teeth. The rosy flowers grow in groups or panicles; and the fruit, red and ripening to rich purple, is full of juice that man has used since recorded time. The Israeli bramble is the blackberry bush, common also in European countrysides. In the East, the Arabs burn it for fuel, hacking it down with sharp, curved sickles.

Bramble Rubus ulmifolius   Hebrew: atâd
Then said all the trees unto the bramble, Come thou, and reign over.

                                                        JUDGES 9:14

Bulrush

---

*And Pharaoh charged all his people, saying,
Every son that is born ye shall cast into the river,
and every daughter ye shall save alive. . . . a
daughter of Levi . . . bare a son: and when she
saw him that he was a goodly child, she hid him
three months. And when she could not longer
hide him, she took for him an ark of bulrushes,
and daubed it with slime and with pitch, and
put the child therein; and she laid it in the flags
by the river's bank.* EXODUS 1:22, 2:1, 2, 3

The miraculous saving of the child Moses was one of the most
heart-warming episodes of the Old Testament. He was laid in a
cradle woven from the bulrushes of papyrus growing so
prolifically in the rivers of lower Egypt, and among these same
bulrushes the ark was placed, to be discovered almost at once by
Pharaoh's daughter who brought Moses up as her own son. The
bulrush was very common in ancient Egypt, and in certain areas
completely covered the surface of the Nile. It is a beautiful and
graceful plant, with a large and very heavy root that protects it
from being swept away in the floods. From this root grow trian-
gular stems reaching a great height and bearing at the top a plume
of fine stalks resembling feathers. On these stalks grow clusters of
little brown rushlike flowers that produce the seeds. Papyrus provided the earliest known material for the making of paper, which
gets its name from the plant. The Arabs call it *babeer*. They also
collect its roots to burn as fuel. The writing material of the old
Egyptians was made by using the pith of the stems, laid flat and
glued together. Then the whole mass was pressed under heavy
weights, and when dry it was ready to be written on. The first
paint brushes were fashioned from this reed by fraying the ends
of the stalks.

Bulrush Cyperus papyrus   Hebrew: gômeh
  . . . *she took for him an ark of bulrushes* . . . EXODUS 2:3

Camphire

---

*My beloved is unto me as a cluster of camphire
in the vineyards of Engedi.*

SONG OF SOLOMON 1:14

*Thy plants are an orchard of pomegranates, with
pleasant fruits; camphire, with spikenard.*

SONG OF SOLOMON 4:13

One of the earliest known spices and perfumes is the camphire or henna flower, here lauded by King Solomon for its beautiful fragrance. Sometimes called the cypress flower, it is also the *alhenna* of the Arabs. It has creamy white, highly scented blossoms, hanging in clusters like grapes, and grows in Israel, Egypt, Arabia, and most of the northern parts of Africa. The henna, reaching a height of ten feet, is much valued, especially by the women of Egypt, for it yields a powerful dye of a dark dusky red, rather like iron rust in color. The women use it to stain the palms of their hands and soles of their feet. It is also an effective check to excessive perspiration. Camphire has been traded for centuries, a fact substantiated by evidence found on mummies entombed for three thousand years that still retain the dye used in life on their nails. The small tree has leaves similar to the olive, but greener and softer, and protruding from the little bell-like flowers are many stamens that impart a light and feathery appearance. When the leaves are pounded, they provide a violent yellow stain for the hair and beard. The seeds, when ripened, are black. Today, as in the time of Solomon, the camphire luxuriates by the Dead Sea at Engedi.

Camphire Lawsonia inermis   Hebrew: côpher

. . . with pleasant fruits; camphire, with spikenard.

SONG OF SOLOMON 4:13

Cassia

Moreover the Lord spake unto Moses, saying,
Take thou also unto thee principal spices, . . .
of cassia five hundred shekels, after the shekel of
the sanctuary, and of oil olive an hin: and thou
shalt make it an oil of holy ointment, an ointment
compound after the art of the apothecary: it
shall be an holy anointing oil.

EXODUS 30: 22, 23, 24, 25

The holy shekel, as mentioned in EXODUS 30: 13, was a full and just shekel, a shekel of the sanctuary according to temple standards. It was an ancient Babylonian weight, approximately half an ounce. Thus was the cassia weighed and valued before it was mixed with the principal spices of the oil of the holy anointing. The cassia of the Scriptures bears the Hebrew name *kiddah*, meaning a bark that peels off. It is a fragrant tree much resembling the cinnamon, though less delicate in taste and perfume. Although the bark is thicker and coarser, it is not so expensive and is frequently mixed with other spices. Buds of the tree are used in place of cloves to season dishes for the table. The smaller leaves provide the medicine known as senna leaves, and are dispensed as Alexandria senna or Aleppo senna. Pods of cassia are also added to the leaves to compound a purgative substance known as cathartin. In rich supply, it was one of the chief articles of commerce at Tyre. "*. . . thou that art situate at the entry of the sea, which art a merchant of the people for many isles, . . . Dan also and Javan going to and fro occupied in thy fairs: bright iron, cassia, and calamus, were in thy market.*" EZEKIEL 27: 3, 19.

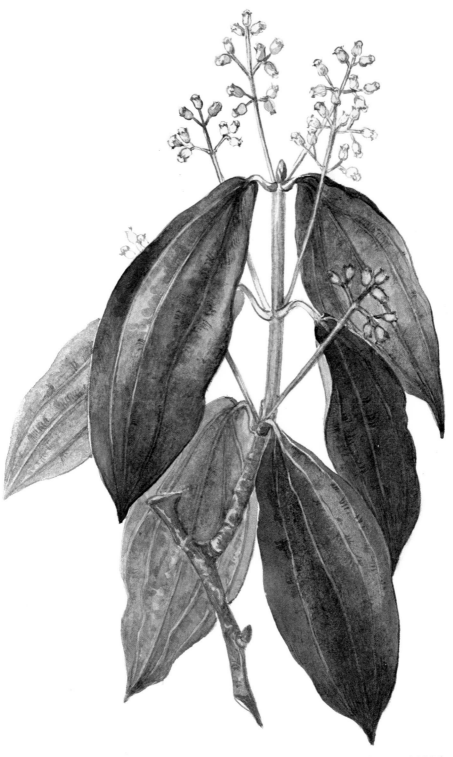

Cassia Cinnamomum cassia   Hebrew: kiddah

     . . . cassia, and calamus, were in thy market. EZEKIEL 27:19

Cedar

And the Lord spake unto Moses and unto Aaron, saying, . . . Speak unto the children of Israel, that they bring thee a red heifer without spot, wherein is no blemish, and upon which never came yoke . . . and the priest shall take cedar wood, and hyssop, and scarlet, and cast it into the midst of the burning of the heifer.

NUMBERS 19: 1, 2, 6

The word in the Hebrew is taken from an old Arabic derivation meaning a firmly rooted, strong tree. It signifies also that this tree is long-lived, and very slow-growing. This is a cedar that is found in Syria. It is native also to the plains of Galilee and Gilead, and can live on high desolate mountains, in rocky isolation, where only wild goats and gazelles can make their way safely. This species is the brown-berried cedar, or juniper, but the fruit is more orange than brown, and measures half an inch across. Referred to also as the sharp cedar, it attains a height of twenty feet, and has firm, glistening foliage. It was the cedar used for sacrificial duty in the Temple, and used by the priests at the altar on all occasions and festivals.

Cedar Juniperus oxycedrus   Hebrew: erez
And the priest shall take cedar wood . . . NUMBERS 19:6

Cedar of Lebanon

Behold, . . . a cedar in Lebanon with fair branches, and with a shadowing shroud, and of an high stature; and his top was among the thick boughs. . . . Therefore his height was exalted above all the trees of the field, and his boughs were multiplied, and his branches became long because of the multitude of waters, when he shot forth. EZEKIEL 31:3, 5

This is a description of the magnificence of the greatest of all the trees of the Holy Land celebrated in the Scriptures. It is a noble evergreen, often one hundred and twenty feet tall and forty feet in girth, with branches that shoot horizontally from the trunk some ten feet from the ground. The tree bears a cone that takes three years to mature. First it is tiny and pale green; the second year it reaches its full size of nearly three inches, but is still not ripe; the third season it turns a rich brown and scatters its seeds, which are minute, considering the size of the tree. Today this cedar grows wild only in Turkey, Lebanon, and Syria, but many handsome specimens are cultivated in England and France. It exudes a gum or balsam which makes the wood so fragrant that to walk in a grove of cedars is a delight. Some specimens of cedar of Lebanon are judged to be two thousand years old. Many younger trees are now taking their places among them. The wood is particularly adaptable for building, since it does not quickly decay, nor is it eaten by insect larvae. It is of a beautiful warm red tone, solid, and free from knots. Therefore it was used in building the Temple at Jerusalem, as well as Solomon's palace, known as "the house of the forest of Lebanon" because of the quantity of this wood used in its construction.

Cedar of Lebanon Cedrus libani   Hebrew: erez

*The righteous shall flourish like the palm tree: he shall grow
like a cedar in Lebanon.*   PSALMS 92:12

Chesnut (plane tree)

. . . and the chesnut trees were not like his branches; nor any tree in the garden of God was like unto him in his beauty. EZEKIEL 31:8

The tree here termed "chesnut" is identified by the Septuagint and the Vulgate as the "plane tree," a determination with which most modern students agree. It has a tall and stately trunk with a smooth bark, and branches spreading in every direction. The glossy, vinelike leaves are of a rich dark green; its fruits, in the form of small globes, are covered with little spikes. Nowhere is it to be found in greater abundance than on the plains of Assyria and in Israel, where it thrives along the borders of streams and edges of rivers. On the Mediterranean coast it is planted for its shade; under its branches Socrates held his audiences enthralled by his wisdom. Avenues of planes were planted in Athens and other Greek cities. The Hebrew name *armon* means "naked" as well as "peeling off," and this no doubt refers to the peeling off of the bark each year. Pliny refers to the immense size of the tree. One plane tree near Istanbul is thought to be over two thousand years old.

(48)

Chesnut (plane tree) Platanus orientalis   Hebrew: armôn
And Jacob took him rods of green poplar, and of the hazel and
chesnut tree . . .   GENESIS 30:37

Cinnamon

And the merchants of the earth shall weep and mourn over her; for no man buyeth their merchandise any more: . . . all manner vessels of most precious wood . . . and cinnamon, and odours, and ointments. . . . The merchants of these things, which were made rich by her, shall stand afar off for the fear of her torment, weeping and wailing. . . .

REVELATION 18:11, 12, 13, 15

The dramatic fall of the Antichrist's kingdom is here foretold, and among its precious commodities is enumerated the cinnamon. EXODUS 30:23, 25, 26 records that the Lord said to Moses, *"Take thou also unto thee principal spices, of pure myrrh five hundred shekels, and of sweet cinnamon half so much . . . and thou shalt make it an oil of holy ointment. . . . And thou shalt anoint the tabernacle of the congregation therewith. . . ."* The cinnamon belongs to the laurel family, and grows to thirty feet high. Its leaves are very stiff and evergreen, and the flowers, which are a quarter of an inch long, are yellowish-white and grouped in silky clusters. Native to Sri Lanka, it is known there as *kornuda ganah*. For centuries its source was kept a close secret by Arabs who first carried it to the world's markets. The tree yields a spice that has been in continuous use since the early days of Greece and Rome. Commercial cinnamon is obtained from the inner bark, and the shoots or branches, one inch thick, are cut when this bark peels easily. Then the strips are wrapped around a thin rod, and the outer skin scraped off. Quills of cinnamon are sold commercially. They are golden brown and have a pungent, yet very pleasant aromatic taste.

Cinnamon Cinnamomum zeylanicum   Hebrew: kinnamon

. . . cinnamon, with all trees of frankincense . . .

SONG OF SOLOMON 4:14

Cockle

If my land cry against me, or that the furrows likewise thereof complain; if I have eaten the fruits thereof without money, . . . let thistles grow instead of wheat, and cockle instead of barley. . . . JOB 31:38, 39, 40

Here Job made a solemn protestation of his integrity and just dealing, and invited punishment to be sent to him should his words have been not just and true. The cockle he talked of is a beautiful sturdy plant about four feet high, native to the Mediterranean region. The flower, one and a half inches across, is a vivid rose pink, heavily veined, and bears black markings. The plant's growth is branching, and the stalks are covered with a gray down. The calyx grows larger to hold the hard, brown seed capsule. This plant, however, is a noxious weed, introducing itself into wheat and barley fields. The seeds are a great irritant to the human system, poisonous if ground with flour. Unless the latter is well sifted, the seeds will turn the whole mass bitter. However, the flower has been used in past centuries, especially by the Romans, for the weaving of chaplets. Guests attending feasts and games in the arenas were handed a coronet of these flowers to place on their brows.

Cockle Agrostemma githago   Hebrew: boshah

Let thistles grow instead of wheat, and cockle instead of barley.

JOB 31:40

Coriander

*But now our soul is dried away: there is nothing
at all, beside this manna, before our eyes. And
the manna was as coriander seed. . . . And the
people went about, and gathered it, and ground
it in mills, or beat it in a mortar, and baked it in
pans, and made cakes of it: and the taste of it was
as the taste of fresh oil. And when the dew fell
upon the camp in the night, the manna fell upon
it.* NUMBERS 11:6, 7, 8, 9

The Israelites were on the march from Sinai to Paran, their hopes
on the Promised Land in the far distance. When they became
hungry and cried out for food, the Lord God sent them manna
from heaven, similar to coriander seed. The coriander is an um-
belliferous plant, with leaves like parsley. It is part of the carrot
family, but is distinct from the true carrot in that the seeds or
fruits are rounded and gray and the size of a peppercorn. They
have a sharp though pleasant aroma. The Arabs find it a wholesome spice, as do the Egyptians and Indians who add it to their
meat. It grows wild in Egypt and Israel, and can be found in
China. Bread in the East is flavored with coriander and confec-
tioners in Europe add it to their baked cakes and sweetmeats.
Seeds planted in March or early spring send up the annual stem to
a height of twenty-four inches. The flowers are white or pinkish,
and the leaves are finely cut. The seeds contain a valuable oil
which provides the flavoring. Common and available in Israel, the
plant was used as early as 1550 B.C. for culinary and medicinal
purposes. This fact is substantiated by records found in the
papyrus of Ebers and in the writings of Cato and Pliny.

Coriander Coriandrum sativum   Hebrew: gad

. . . *it was like coriander seed* . . . EXODUS 16:31

Cotton

And when these days were completed, the king gave for all the people present in Susa the capital, both great and small a banquet lasting for seven days, in the court of the garden of the king's palace. There were white cotton curtains and blue hangings caught up with cords of fine linen and purple to silver rings and marble pillars. . . .

ESTHER 1:5, 6, R.S.V.

Only once in the Holy Scriptures is cotton mentioned, and this is in the account of the hall in which the feast was given by King Ahasuerus to all his princes and their servants and to the nobles and princes of the provinces. According to Pasanius, who recorded events in 480 B.C., cotton was cultivated in his part of the Holy Land, Judea, and was yellower than that of Egypt. There is no doubt that cotton materials were known to the Jews while they were held captive in Persia under King Ahasuerus, who was monarch over the provinces from India to Ethiopia. That cotton was used as clothing has been proved by the minute examination of the cloths in which the Egyptian mummies were wrapped. The word "calico," a cotton fabric, came from Calicut, India; "muslin" from Mosul in Asiatic Turkey; and "nankeen" from Nankin. Spinning and weaving were known to the women of the Holy Land, who brought what they had spun for service in the Temple. Jesus promised his people that the worthy shall be clothed in white raiment. The bush that bears the cotton grows about sixty inches high. It has creamy yellow or sometimes pink flowers, and the leaves are deeply lobed. The seed vessel forms after the flower petals die off, and remains on the stem until quite ripe. Then it bursts and the cotton swells out from the boll in fluffy masses. It is passed through a gin to comb it, then finally processed and woven into the fabric known as cotton.

Cotton Gossypium herbaceum   Hebrew: karpas

There were white cotton curtains and blue hangings . . .

ESTHER 1:6 (RSV)

Cucumber

. . . and the children of Israel also wept again, and said, Who shall give us flesh to eat? We remember the fish, which we did eat in Egypt freely; the cucumbers. . . . But now our soul is dried away. . . . NUMBERS 11:4, 5, 6

Here we read of the trials of the children of Israel, when at length they had left Egypt. With their leader Moses, they were now in the wilderness of Paran and on their way to the Promised Land. Throughout the great heat of summer they longed for the refreshment of the cooling fruits so much enjoyed in Egypt. The cucumber was one delicacy they constantly desired. It was extensively grown in Egypt and Palestine, more abundantly in the former country. Thick, moist mud found along the banks of the Nile is perfect for raising this plant, while the hot sun brings especially swift growth. The fruit is an important food for the poor, and a gratifying relish in the heat. The cucumber today is similar to the one grown in biblical times. Its color is rich blue-green, the flowers are white and of a pretty shape, and the growth is low and rambling as it straggles over the ground. ISAIAH 1:8 records: *"The daughter of Zion is left . . . as a lodge in a garden of cucumbers, as a besieged city."* The lodge, a crude hut of four poles and walls of woven boughs, housed the watchman who protected the plants. In Hebrew a garden of cucumbers is *mikshah*.

Cucumber Cucumis sativus   Hebrew: kishuîm
   . . . *the cucumbers, and the melons, and the leeks, and the onions,*
and the garlick . . .   NUMBERS 11:5

Cummin

For his God doth instruct him to discretion, and doth teach him. For the fitches are not threshed with a threshing instrument, neither is a cart wheel turned about upon the cummin; but the fitches are beaten out with a staff, and the cummin with a rod. ISAIAH 28:26, 27

The prophet Isaiah impressed upon the children of Judah that the loving-kindness of their God extended to them, and even to the sowing and harvesting of the smallest seeds created for their use. This little plant, the cummin, rises to twelve inches in height, has finely cut leaves, and dainty pink or white flowers forming umbels at the tops of very much branched stems. It is the only species of its genus, and western Asia is its home. Cummin is not found wild at all; it has been cultivated from earliest times. The fruit is the valuable part of the plant, its medicinal properties having been known to the ancients far back in history. Centuries ago, Persia raised the plant for the seeds. Similar in shape to the fennel, it contains a valuable oil that is strongly aromatic. When used as a spice, it is crushed and mixed with bread and added to the meat pot. Kammon, a village near Acre, takes its name from the Hebrew word for this flower, and for the sharp smell abounding there. The fruit is rounded and dry, and harvested by beating the stalks with a rod. This method preserves the small and tender seeds that would be ruined if threshed otherwise. Cummin is again mentioned in the Bible when Jesus reproved the scribes: "*Woe unto you, scribes and Pharisees, hypocrites! for ye pay tithe of mint . . . and cummin, and have omitted the weightier matters of the law, judgment, mercy, and faith; these ought ye to have done. . . .*" MATTHEW 23:23.

Cummin Cuminum cyminum   Hebrew: cammôn
    . . . *but the fitches are beaten out with a staff, and the cummin*
    with a rod.   ISAIAH 28:27

Cypress

---

*The carpenter stretcheth out his rule; he mark-
eth it out with a line. . . . He heweth him down
cedars, and taketh the cypress and the oak,
which he strengtheneth for himself among the
trees of the forest. . . .* ISAIAH 44:13, 14

Ten species of this outstanding tree are known in the Northern
Hemisphere. The Apocrypha states that it grows upon the mountains of Hermon, while explorers record that it is the only tree
that can live at the summit of Mount Lebanon. One kind of cypress is tall with erect close branches. An elegant slender form is a
favorite with Moslems and Armenians who plant the tree in
their burial grounds. Cypress wood is hard and fragrant, with a
beautiful reddish hue that never disappears. It was made into
winepresses, rafters, and joists, and even the decks of ships. St.
Peter's Church in Rome had two large doors carved from it; these
lasted in position for six hundred years, when they were replaced
by two of brass. Authorities accept the statement that cypress
was the wood selected by Noah to construct the ark: "*Make thee
an ark of gopher wood; rooms shalt thou make in the ark, and shalt
pitch it within and without with pitch. . . . The length of the
ark shall be three hundred cubits, the breadth of it fifty cubits,
and the height of it thirty cubits. . . . Thus did Noah; according
to all that God commanded him, so did he.*" GENESIS 6:14, 15, 22.
Scholars have investigated the possibility that the ark still remains
on Mount Ararat in Turkey.

Cypress Cupressus sempervirens var. horizontalis   Hebrew: tirzah

He heweth him down cedars, and taketh the cypress and the oak . . .

ISAIAH 44:14

Desire (caper)

Also when they shall be afraid of that which is high, and fears shall be in the way, and the almond tree shall flourish, and the grasshopper shall be a burden, and desire shall fail: because man goeth to his long home, and the mourners go about the streets: . . . Then shall the dust return to the earth as it was: and the spirit shall return unto God who gave it. ECCLESIASTES 12:5, 7

Here is spoken the realism of advancing age about the loss of the senses that delight the man in youth. Taste and appetite are among the first to leave the aging man, and a stimulant to these was provided by the caper. On the Arabian peninsula this small yet most conspicuous plant is known as *asuf*. It is common in Egypt and the Sinai peninsula and can be found in the rocky clefts of the mountains where it is often so prevalent that the gorges are filled with the rich green of its leaves. It has a trailing habit of growth, and along its long horizontal stem leaves are borne at regular intervals. Where the leaves join the main stem are two recurved spiny thorns from which the plant gets its older scientific name. The flower appears in May and is pure white, two to three inches broad, with wide open petals. From the center of the flower arises a cluster of rose-magenta filaments with golden yellow tips, and one long green pistil shoots through the midst of them. It is the young pickled buds of the caper that give the "desire" or relish to food. Today in the Mediterranean islands they are still gathered and steeped in casks of vinegar for an appetizer. The caper also bears a large inedible berry two and a half inches long. In the King James Version of the Ecclesiastes text the translation is "*desire shall fail*," but the original Hebrew reads that "*the caper berry shall fail*." The Talmud refers to it as *kafrisin*.

(64)

Desire (caper) Capparis spinosa   Hebrew: tapher
  . . . *the grasshopper shall be a burden, and desire shall fail* . . .
                                        ECCLESIASTES 12:5

Dove's Dung
(star of Bethlehem)

And there was a great famine in Samaria: and, behold, they besieged it, until an ass's head was sold for fourscore pieces of silver, and the fourth part of a cab of dove's dung for five pieces of silver   II KINGS 6:25

This is the story describing the siege of Samaria in all its graphic realism. The dove's dung here represented is the bulb of the lovely little white flower growing so abundantly in the springtime throughout the Holy Land. Literally translated, the first part of its Latin name means "bird's milk." The stalk attains a height of six inches, and the ribbon leaves are long and clear green. It was the bulb that was so valued in times of stress and starvation. Dug up and dried, it could be eaten roasted, or ground to flour and mixed with meal to make bread. Even today in Italy these bulbs are cooked and eaten like chestnuts. For centuries the Syrians have used this bulb as food. Dioscorides, the historian, writes that in his time this bulb was dried and added to flour to make thin cakes. Its worth was high in time of famine. The people relieved their hunger by utilizing the little plant known then, as now, as dove's dung. The cab referred to was a Hebrew measure amounting to three and one third pints and priced at twenty pieces of silver. This amount of the precious metal, when weighed in odd lumps, equaled the weight of the cab. At that era in Bible history no coinage had yet been struck for commercial transactions.

Dove's Dung (star of Bethlehem) Ornithogalum umbellatum

Hebrew: chiryonim

. . . *and the fourth part of a cab of dove's dung for five pieces of silver.*   II KINGS 6:25

Ebony

The men of Dedan were thy merchants; many isles were the merchandise of thine hand: they brought thee for a present horns of ivory and ebony. EZEKIEL 27:15

Ebony is mentioned this once in the Bible. It was not unknown, however, for it was valued even in remotest times, and much used in the manufacture of fine furniture. This passage is an account of the great wealth of Tyre, and of the peoples who went there to trade, many of them coming from as far as the Persian Gulf. Ebony was costly and was the heartwood of certain trees native to Ceylon and southern India. These grow to great size, and have a smooth bark covering a white soft sapwood that is of no value, and a good trunk can be cut to yield a black heartwood log two feet in diameter and ten to fifteen feet long. This is a valuable commodity, for it is hard, heavy, and durable and will take a glistening polish. It has been long been used with the native ivory to make inlaid objects of striking appearance. Herodotus records that the Ethiopians were called upon to deliver tribute to the Persians in the form of ebony and pure gold. Because of its hardness, ebony takes its name from the Hebrew word *eben*, a stone. Also, the name Ebenezer means literally "stone of my help." The ebony tree bears large stout leaves nearly four inches long, and small cream-colored flowers in the shape of bells. In Old Testament days it was brought to the Holy Land from India, and carried in ships up the Red Sea.

Ebony Diospyros ebenaster   Hebrew: hobnim

. . . they brought thee for a present horns of ivory and ebony.

EZEKIEL 27:15

Fig Tree

And when the woman saw that the tree was good for food, . . . and a tree to be desired to make one wise, she took of the fruit thereof, and did eat, and gave also unto her husband with her; and he did eat. And the eyes of them both were opened, and they knew that they were naked; and they sewed fig leaves together, and made themselves aprons. GENESIS 3:6, 7

The fig is the first of the fruits to be named in the Bible; its leaves were used to make a covering for Adam and his wife Eve in the Garden of Eden. Although the fig is not a large tree, there are some growing near Jenin that reach the height of twenty-five feet. It is a beautiful tree for providing shade, and its Hebrew name means "to spread out." To sit under one's own vine and fig tree was the Jewish concept of peace and prosperity as indicated in I KINGS 4:25. The fruit often appears before the leaves, but the flowers are never conspicuous. They are all enclosed in a large hollow receptacle, and would never produce seeds but for the visit of a little fig wasp, a mere one eighth of an inch long, that enters and fertilizes the blossoms. The figs are eaten fresh in Israel, though when they are taken on journeys they have been dried and threaded on long strings. "Cakes of figs" are mentioned in I SAMUEL 25:18, and these also were for eating when traveling. Fig leaves are still sewn together in the East; they are used by natives as wrappings for fresh fruit sent to the markets. To the Egyptians the fig tree represented the Tree of Life. One of their goddesses presented figs to mortals who were thought worthy of eternal happiness. Bethphage or "house of unripe figs" is a town on the Mount of Olives, famous in ancient times for this fruit.

Fig Tree Ficus carica   Hebrew: teenah
   Whoso keepeth the fig tree shall eat the fruit thereof . . .
                              PROVERBS 27:18

Fir (Aleppo pine)

The glory of Lebanon shall come unto thee, the fir tree, the pine tree, and the box together, to beautify the place of my sanctuary; and I will make the place of my feet glorious. . . . and all they that despised thee shall bow themselves down at the soles of thy feet; and they shall call thee, The city of the Lord, The Zion of the Holy One of Israel. ISAIAH 60:13, 14

In the Holy Land the fir, translated "pine" by botanical authorities, was an emblem of nobility and great stature. Several varieties of pines grow on Mount Lebanon, the largest being the Aleppo pine. It is a lofty tree, attaining a height of sixty feet. The silver-gray bark is smooth and the leaves, or needles, grow in pairs. The cones are red-brown and polished, four to five inches long, turning grayish when they open. They then drop the small seeds contained inside. For centuries the timber of this fine cone-bearing tree has been used for beams or rafters in temples and houses, as evidenced in I KINGS 5:10. Throughout the Crusades there was an entire forest of these pines between Jerusalem and Bethlehem. The fir is the commonest tree of its type on the western side of the river Jordan. Resins of firs and pines were well known to the ancients; an essential oil or turpentine was used in the "Greek fire" of medieval warfare.

Fir (Aleppo pine) Pinus halepensis   Hebrew: berôsh

. . . and I will cut down . . . the choice fir trees thereof . . .

ISAIAH 37:24

Fitches

Give ye ear, and hear my voice; hearken, and hear my speech. Doth the plowman plow all day to sow? doth he open and break the clods of his ground? When he hath made plain the face thereof, doth he not cast abroad the fitches . . . ? For his God doth instruct him to discretion, and doth teach him. For the fitches are not threshed with a threshing instrument, . . . but the fitches are beaten out with a staff. . . .
ISAIAH 28:23, 24, 25, 26, 27

God had instructed man even in small details. The smaller seeds sown for man's use were harvested in a special way. A light staff or cane was used for the fitches, as they were too small for a threshing instrument. This plant is known as the fennel or nutmeg flower, and authorities have decided that the biblical fitches are its seeds. The plant grows two feet high, and bears a lovely cerulean blue flower, with five green curling pistils and many stamens tipped with black anthers. As the biblical reference truly indicates, its seeds can be separated from the husks with very little trouble. The feathery leaves are very pretty, clear green, and finely divided. When the flower fades, the seed vessel forms. Inside it is divided into cells that keep quantities of the seed separated; the outer covering is easily whipped off. The tiny seeds are very hot to the palate, and are sprinkled on food like pepper; in fact, in Europe they are sometimes mixed with real pepper. They are also added to bread and sprinkled on cakes. In the East the plant is cultivated for commercial purposes.

Fitches Nigella sativa   Hebrew: ketzah

For the fitches are not threshed with a threshing instrument . . .

ISAIAH 28:27

Flax

And the king of Jericho sent unto Rahab, saying,
Bring forth the men that are come to thee, which
are entered into thine house: for they be come to
search out all the country. And the woman took
the two men, . . . and hid them with the stalks
of flax, which she had laid in order upon the
roof.   JOSHUA 2:3, 4, 6

Rahab used the flax to hide Joshua's spies from the king of
Jericho. The flax plant is commonly used to make linen, the most
ancient of all textile fibers. It was in cultivation before the arrival
of the children of Israel into Canaan. Flax grows thirty-six inches
high, and is found in many lands. Its flowers have five petals and
are a beautiful blue, with a violet marking at the base. The leaves
are narrow, and the whole plant is very dainty. In early times the
crop was pulled up by the roots and laid flat to dry; the stems
were then steeped in water until the outer part decayed. Next,
these were split and combed until the useful threads separated and
peeled off from the stalk. This process is known as retting. The
spindle and distaff were used to separate the fine thread, ready to
be woven into linen. Moses spoke of the fine linen of Egypt and
of its superior excellence. The infant Jesus' swaddling clothes
were most probably made of linen, as were his burial clothes.
"And, behold, there was a man named Joseph, a counsellor; and
he was a good man, and a just: . . . This man went unto Pilate,
and begged the body of Jesus. And he took it down, and wrapped
it in linen, and laid it in a sepulchre. . . ." LUKE 23:50, 52, 53.

Flax Linum usitatissimum   Hebrew: pishtah
She seeketh wool, and flax, and worketh willingly with her hands.

PROVERBS 31:13

Frankincense

---

*When they saw the star, they rejoiced with ex-
ceeding great joy. And when they were come
into the house, they saw the young child with
Mary his mother, and fell down, and worshipped
him: and when they had opened their treasures,
they presented unto him gifts; gold, and frankincense, and myrrh.*   MATTHEW 2:10, 11

The wise men from the East had traveled for many months to
reach Jerusalem. There they inquired, saying, "*Where is he that
is born King of the Jews? for we have seen his star in the east, and
are come to worship him.*" MATTHEW 2:2. They had brought
three gifts of great value: the first was gold, in token of kingship;
then frankincense for holiness; and myrrh to symbolize the
suffering the newborn infant would have to endure in his life on
earth. The frankincense tree is found in the Himalayas in India,
and also in the northern part of the Arabian peninsula. It is a
handsome tree, bearing clear green leaves like the mountain ash,
and pretty star-shaped pink flowers with lemon centers. The
wood is heavy, hard, and durable, and is used for many purposes.
At the end of February the Arabs cut the bark and peel off a thin
layer. A month later this process is repeated, and then the juice or
resin flows out from the inner wood. This, when it has hardened,
becomes brittle, glittering, and bitter to the taste, and is recognized as the finest burning resin, or incense, in the world; hence
its name frank-incense, or "free lighting." It is mentioned many
times in the Bible in relation to the worship in the Temple; it
was also burned for fumigation when beasts were offered for
sacrifice. *Libanum* is the frankincense of the ancients, and *Luban*
signified "Milk of the Arabs."

Frankincense Boswellia thurifera   Hebrew: lebonah

. . . they presented unto him gifts; gold, and frankincense, and myrrh.   MATTHEW 2:11

Galbanum

---

*And the Lord said unto Moses, Take unto thee
sweet spices, stacte, and onycha, and galbanum;
these sweet spices with pure frankincense: of
each shall there be a like weight: And thou shalt
make it a perfume, a confection after the art of
the apothecary, tempered together, pure and
holy: And thou shalt beat some of it very small,
and put of it before the testimony in the tabernacle of the congregation, where I will meet
with thee: it shall be unto you most holy.*

EXODUS 30: 34, 35, 36

Thus the galbanum was selected to be an ingredient in the incense
burned at the golden altar in the Holy Place. It is the gum of the
plant *Ferula galbaniflua* that grows from Syria to Iran. Pliny
knew it as *stagonites*. In Singhalese it is called *perunkayam*, and in
Sanskrit *hingu*. It is a fetid yellowish gum resin, containing a
chemical substance called umbelliferone. In biblical times the
product was imported. Nine species of *Ferula* grow in the area of
Israel. The plant is a strong-rooted perennial, its stem reaching
several feet in height. The leaves are finely divided, and the
umbels are composed of small greenish-white flowers. When it is
ripe, the gum is collected by cutting the young stem a few inches
above the ground. A milky juice flows out and very soon hardens. When this is burned, the odor is pungent and pleasant.
Today it is used in the manufacture of varnish; the drug asafoe-
tida is also obtained from it.

(80)

Galbanum Ferula galbaniflua   Hebrew: chalbenah

. . . Take unto thee sweet spices, stacte, and onycha, and galbanum . . .   EXODUS 30:34

Gall

---

*And as they came out, they found a man of Cy-
rene, Simon by name: him they compelled to
bear his cross. And when they were come unto a
place called Golgotha, . . . they gave him vinegar to drink mingled with gall: and when he had
tasted thereof, he would not drink.*

MATTHEW 27:32, 33, 34

The gall that was added to the vinegar and offered to Jesus was
the juice of the opium poppy, a flower thriving in Israel. The
plant provides a narcotic that induces sleep, a sleep so heavy that
the person becomes insensible. When the Roman soldiers at Golgotha took pity on their prisoner on the cross, they added this
poppy juice to the potion of vinegar. Jesus tasted the mixture but
refused it, resolving to suffer so that the Father's plan of redemp-
tion might be fulfilled. Opium is one of the most valuable drugs,
and is obtained from the gall plant by making horizontal incisions
in the poppy heads that are the seed vessels. This incising is done
a few days after the flower petals have fallen. A milky juice then
exudes in long drops, and solidifies in twenty-four hours. The
flower is particularly beautiful, clear lavender or white, with a
heavy stain of rich purple at the base of each of the four petals. It
grows waist-high, and its foliage is silvery blue-green.

Gall Papaver somniferum   Hebrew: rôsh

They gave him vinegar to drink mingled with gall . . . MATTHEW 27:34

Garlic

We remember the fish, which we did eat in
Egypt freely; the cucumbers, and the melons,
and the leeks, and the onions, and the garlick:
But now our soul is dried away: there is nothing
at all, beside this manna, before our eyes. . . .
And Moses said unto the Lord, . . . Whence
should I have flesh to give unto all this people?
for they weep unto me, saying, Give us flesh,
that we may eat. I am not able to bear all this
people alone, because it is too heavy for me.

NUMBERS 11:5, 6, 11, 13, 14

This is the only verse in the Bible mentioning the vegetables that
were constantly missed by the Israelites during their journey to-
ward the Promised Land. Garlic was one of the staple foods in
Egypt, where it grew in great abundance. There are several species. The bulbs are almost round, and composed of several fleshy
layers. Smaller bulblets known as cloves of garlic grow around
the main one: these can be separated, and each one is large enough
to add flavor to a meat dish. The clear green leaves are long and
ribbonlike. The flowers burst through a sheath to form a globe of
blossoms, each floweret bearing six similar sepals and petals. In
one of the Egyptian pyramids is an inscription stating that one
hundred thousand men were employed for thirty years in its construction. These laborers ate garlic, leeks, and onions, to the value
of sixteen hundred talents of silver. Pliny notes that divine honors
were paid to garlic, and that the Egyptians placed it among their
deities.

Garlic Allium sativum   Hebrew: shum
We remember . . . the garlick . . . NUMBERS 11:5

Goodly Fruit

Also in the fifteenth day of the seventh month,
when ye have gathered in the fruit of the land,
ye shall keep a feast unto the Lord seven days: on
the first day shall be a sabbath, and on the eighth
day shall be a sabbath. And ye shall take you on
the first day the boughs of goodly trees, branches
of palm trees, and the boughs of thick trees, and
willows of the brook; and ye shall rejoice before
the Lord your God seven days.

LEVITICUS 23:39, 40

The law required that during the celebration of the feast of the fruit harvest every Israelite should carry branches of the citron, or goodly fruit, to symbolize God's gift of fruits. Josephus records that this citron grew on the boughs of the "goodly trees." To this day it is carried in the hand at the autumn feast. The citron is native to India, but has been grown in Palestine for centuries. It is a shrublike tree, often attaining a height of ten feet, with irregular, straggling, thick branches and a gray-white bark. Its flowers are similar to those of the orange and are equally beautiful; the petals are thick and fleshy, backed with rose, and the center is crowded with golden stamens. The blossoms yield a heavy fruit known as *malus medea*, and "citron of Assyria." It is believed by many people to be the forbidden fruit of the Garden of Eden; hence it is also known as *pomum adami*. Gerard, the English herbalist, describes it thus: "Assyrian apple tree. The fruit is as large as a cucumber set with divers knobs or bumps, and of a very pleasant smell, and it has sour juice and seeds as large as barley."

(86)

Goodly Fruit Citrus medica   Hebrew: etz hadar

And ye shall take you on the first day the boughs of goodly trees . . .

LEVITICUS 23:40

Gourd

So Jonah went out of the city, and sat on the east side of the city, and there made him a booth, and sat under it in the shadow, till he might see what would become of the city. And the Lord God prepared a gourd, and made it to come up over Jonah, that it might be a shadow over his head, to deliver him from his grief. So Jonah was exceeding glad of the gourd. But God prepared a worm when the morning rose the next day, and it smote the gourd that it withered.

JONAH 4: 5, 6, 7

This was just another trial, added to the many already borne by the patient prophet, who, according to the Ussher chronology, lived in 825 B.C. The Hebrew word for this plant means "nauseous to the taste." Celsius states that this gourd was the *kharwa* or castor oil tree. It was also identified with the Arabic *el keroa*. The word was derived from the Egyptian *kike*. The plant is a very large bush, ten feet high, with broad handsome leaves of rich green or sometimes bronze that have been likened to the hand of Christ, open and extended in blessing. Flowers form erect spires, each bloom throwing out tiny vermilion sepals among its rich cream anthers. The fruit, at first gray-green, turns to a fiery carmine. From the tree an oil was expressed that was used as fuel for lamps. Pliny records the plant by the shorter name of *kike*. With even slight handling, it can wilt and wither, as did Jonah's when it was destroyed by a worm.

Gourd Ricinus communis   Hebrew: kikayon
So Jonah was exceeding glad of the gourd. JONAH 4:6

Green Bay Tree

I have seen the wicked in great power, and spreading himself like a green bay tree. Yet he passed away, and, lo, he was not: yea, I sought him, but he could not be found. PSALMS 37:35,36

Here was the psalmist foretelling the end of the ungodly man. He used the bay in his analogy because it was symbolic of wealth and wickedness. Translated literally, the Hebrew means simply a tree, "green and vigorous in its native soil." The tree resembles a shrub, the young shoots sprouting from the ground around the parent stem giving it a bushy appearance. Its evergreen leaves, when broken, emit a sweet scent and furnish an extract used by the Orientals in making perfumed oil. The roots and the bark supply a valuable medicine. Creamy white flowers appear in the spring and later ripen into blue-black berries. Today the bay tree grows on the wooded hills of northern Israel and plentifully in the glens near Galilee, as well as on Mount Carmel. It also luxuriates in the old gardens of Tyre and Sidon (now Sur and Saida) and in some areas of North Africa and southern Europe. In the ancient Olympic games the victorious contestant was awarded a chaplet of bay leaves placed on his brow. The Roman gold coin of 342 B.C. has a laurel wreath modeled on its surface.

Green Bay Tree Laurus nobilis   Hebrew: ezrach
  . . . *and spreading himself like a green bay tree.* PSALMS 37:35

Hemlock

*Their heart is divided; now shall they be found
faulty. . . . For now they shall say, We have
no king, because we feared not the Lord. . . .
They have spoken words, swearing falsely in
making a covenant: thus judgment springeth up
as hemlock in the furrows of the field.*

HOSEA 10:2, 3, 4

Hemlock is a dark and poisonous plant. A biennial, it is erect and
branching, reaching five feet in height when well grown. The
root is white, long, and tap-shaped, from which rise hollow and
glossy green stalks. Finely cut leaves resemble a fern, and tiny
white flowers grace the top of the branching stems. Numerous
blood-red blotches on the stem inspired the appellation *maculata*,
meaning spotted. When bruised, the hemlock emits a very disa-
greeable odor. All parts of it, particularly the seeds, contain an
oily substance known as caria. If taken internally by humans, it
acts as an irritant, bringing on paralysis, convulsions, and even
death. Among the ancient Athenians it was administered to pris-
oners given the death penalty, the most famous and fatal potion,
of course, was drunk by Socrates in 399 B.C. Elsewhere in the
Old Testament, Amos, the herdsman, refers to it as an unwhole-
some thing: "*. . . for ye have turned judgment into gall, and the
fruit of righteousness into hemlock.*" AMOS 6:12.

Hemlock Conium maculatum   Hebrew: rôsh

     . . . thus judgment springeth up as hemlock in the furrows of
the field.   HOSEA 10:4

Hyssop (N.T.)

After this, Jesus knowing that all things were now accomplished, that the scripture might be fulfilled, saith, I thirst. Now there was set a vessel full of vinegar: and they filled a spunge with vinegar, and put it upon hyssop, and put it to his mouth.　　JOHN 19:28, 29

The last few moments of Christ's agony on the cross were relieved by moistening his lips with a sponge filled with vinegar. This sponge was raised on a cane of dhura, referred to here as hyssop. It is a tall plant with strong stems, in maturity reaching a height of over six feet. Hyssop is clear yellow-green, and the grains rise out of the wide ribbon-like leaves. These are beautiful when young, and are cut and woven into light portable panniers or baskets. Later the plant turns light buff or fawn, and the foliage dries, then droops on the stalk. Students of the Bible date this grain reed to prehistoric times. In Palestine hyssop is known as "Jerusalem corn," a main and nutritious part of the people's diet. The grains are gathered and ground for meal used in baking coarse bread. A single seed head is of such enormous size that one can supply a meal for a large family. The pith is brittle and dry and hence of no value. It is suggested by some students that the "parched corn" Ruth received from Boaz was the grain of this reed. "*And Boaz said unto her, At mealtime come thou hither, and eat of the bread, and dip thy morsel in the vinegar. . . . and he reached her parched corn, and she did eat, and was sufficed, and left.*" RUTH 2:14.

Hyssop (N.T.) Sorghum vulgare var. durra   Latin: hyssopus
. . . *and they filled a spunge with vinegar, and put it upon hyssop,*
and put it to his mouth.   JOHN 19:29

Hyssop (O.T.)

---

*Then Moses called for all the elders of Israel,
and said unto them, Draw out and take you a
a lamb according to your families, and kill the
passover. And ye shall take a bunch of hyssop,
and dip it in the blood that is in the bason, and
strike the lintel and the two side posts with the
blood that is in the bason; and none of you shall
go out at the door of his house until the morning.*

EXODUS 12:21, 22

This hyssop is a marjoram, in the mint family, native to Egypt. It
is not the Western variety with the blue flowers. The plant has a
hairy stem, strong and wiry, from which shoot out bunches of
golden flowers with small leaves. It holds water very well, and
Moses directed that it be used to flick the blood of the sacrifice
onto the doorposts of the Israelite homes. This was to identify the
Israelites and save them from the death in store for the Egyptians.
*"For the Lord will pass through to smite the Egyptians; and
when he seeth the blood upon the lintel, and on the two side
posts, the Lord will pass over the door, and will not suffer the
destroyer to come in unto your houses to smite you."* EXODUS 12:23.
Hyssop was used in cleansing lepers, as stated in LEVITICUS 14:4:
*"Then shall the priest command to take for him that is to be
cleansed two birds alive and clean, and cedar wood, and scarlet,
and hyssop."* David recognized in it a property for purification,
for he writes: *"Purge me with hyssop, and I shall be clean: wash
me, and I shall be whiter than snow."* PSALMS 51:7.

(96)

Hyssop (O.T.) Origanum maru var. aegyptiacum   Hebrew: ezob
. . . even unto the hyssop that springeth out of the wall . . .

I KINGS 4:33

Judas Tree

*Then Judas, which had betrayed him, when he
saw that he was condemned, repented himself,
and brought again the thirty pieces of silver
. . . And he cast down the pieces of silver in
the temple, and departed, and went and hanged
himself.*   MATTHEW 27:3, 5

The tree from which Judas hanged himself has long been accepted
by authorities as this one that is native to the Mediterranean region. It is a beautiful sight in the springtime, with dense clusters
of rose-pink, pea-shaped blossoms bursting before the leaves appear. In the East, these sweet-tasting flowers added savor to
salads. Eventually the flower clusters turn into a podlike fruit,
pretty but of no value as food. The seeds germinate in two years.
Clear green and heart-shaped leaves are borne on delicate stalks.
The elegant and uncommon foliage resists insects. An old legend
related that the pink flowers blushed rose-red with shame when
Judas chose the tree from which to hang himself. The wood of
this *Cercis* is very hard and beautifully veined, and takes a high
polish. Theophrastus named it *samuda*.

Judas Tree Cercis siliquastrum
. . . *and went and hanged himself.* MATTHEW 27:5

Juniper

---

*And when he saw that, he arose, and went for his
life, and . . . went a day's journey into the
wilderness, and came and sat down under a
juniper tree. . . .*   I KINGS 19:3, 4

Among the flowering shrubs in the Judean wilderness, one of the
most abundant and striking in appearance is the broom—the
flowering broom of the desert—erroneously translated into English as juniper. In Israel it is strictly a desert shrub, spreading
through the Sinai peninsula on to Arabia Petraea. It is a member
of the pea family, with delicate blossoms, white to pale pink,
disposed in pealike clusters. The leaves are very thin and small.
Rodlike and pliant branches resemble osiers and withes, and were
often cut and tied up in bundles used to support growing vines.
The Hebrew word *rothem* means "to bind." Small pods resembling the domestic field pea follow after the flowers. They ripen
to brown, and contain two little rows of peas, small and very bitter. For centuries the broom has provided welcome shade. Vergil
wrote: "Even humble broom and osiers have their uses, and shade
for sleep, and food for flocks produce." The bush makes the
finest charcoal, which burns with intense heat, and the Arabs
maintain that it holds its heat for a whole year. As a fuel it is un-
surpassed in the East, and in the Cairo market fetches a much
higher price than any other kind.

Juniper Retama raetam   Hebrew: rothem

But he . . . came and sat down under a juniper tree . . . I KINGS 19:4

Leeks

And when the people complained, it displeased the Lord: and the Lord heard it; and his anger was kindled. . . . And the people cried unto Moses; . . . and the children of Israel also wept again, and said, . . . We remember the fish, which we did eat in Egypt freely; the cucumbers, and the melons, and the leeks . . . but now our soul is dried away. . . .

NUMBERS 11:1, 2, 4, 5, 6

The leek is yet another of the delectable vegetables that the children of Israel missed while they journeyed through the desert to the Promised Land. It has been a favorite food in Israel from earliest times, and today is consumed in enormous quantities. The Egyptians regarded it as a sacred plant. Pliny writes that the leek was used in compounding thirty-two remedies. It grows upright to a height of over eight inches from a creamy white bulb. The leaves are dark green, and much used in cookery. According to Pliny, the emperor Nero was very fond of leeks and gave the vegetables respectability by having them brought to his table. The leek is the floral emblem of Wales, and has been the chosen badge of the Welsh since their struggle for independence and freedom.

Leeks Allium porrum   Hebrew: chatzir
We remember . . . the leeks . . . NUMBERS 11:5

Lentils

---

*And Jacob sod pottage: and Esau came from the
field, and he was faint: And Esau said to Jacob,
Feed me, I pray thee, with that same red
pottage. . . . Then Jacob gave Esau bread and
pottage of lentiles; and he did eat. . . .*

GENESIS 25:29, 30, 34

The pottage was made from the lentil, a small pea-like plant related to the vetch. Since it can thrive in ground unsuitable to
other seeds, it is grown as a crop all over Syria and in Israel. Soon
after the wheat harvest in June, it is reaped and threshed in similar
fashion. As a food, lentils are mixed with flour and baked into
bread of an inferior quality, or made into a porridge. Augustine
writes that "lentils are used as food in Egypt, for this plant grows
abundantly in that country, which renders the lentils of Alexandria so valuable that they are brought from thence to us, as if
we grew none." The lentil splits into two small hemispheres; the
shape of the convex glasses used for magnification so resembles
the lentil that its Latin name *lens* has been given to these glasses.
Its native country is unknown, though its history is ancient. The
Hebrew *adashim* comes from the word *adeesh*, signifying "to
tend a flock," which would indicate that it is food for peasants
and herdsmen.

Lentils Lens esculenta   Hebrew: adashim
Then Jacob gave Esau bread and pottage of lentiles . . . GENESIS 25:34

Lilies of the Field

Consider the lilies how they grow: they toil not, they spin not; and yet I say unto you, that Solomon in all his glory was not arrayed like one of these.   LUKE 12:27

Many flowers in Israel have been called lilies; in early spring the ground is covered and carpeted with their brilliant blossoms. Jesus was speaking to the multitude near the plain of Gennesaret, a district noted for its masses of color: and more brilliant than all the others then as now was the anemone, or windflower. It grows all along the sides of the roads, ranging in color from glowing crimson to brilliant purple. The plant, growing from a bulb, reaches a height of six inches, has a ruff of fine-cut leaves beneath the blossom, and other fernlike ones around the base of the stem. It springs to life every year after the advent of early rain.

Lilies of the Field Anemone coronaria   Greek: krinon
Consider the lilies of the field, how they grow . . . MATTHEW 6:28

Lily

---

*His cheeks are as a bed of spices, as sweet
flowers: his lips like lilies, dropping sweet smelling myrrh.*   SONG OF SOLOMON 5:13

In the book of Canticles, or Song of Solomon, the lily is especially
favored as a symbol of loveliness; it grew in the gardens of King
Solomon, the regal botanist. According to the Moffatt translation,
a flower of striking beauty is indicated, the color of glowing
flame. The rich red of the chalcedonicum lily, with its perfect
form, fits this description. It has a high stalk of clear green, with
bright and shining leaves, and blossoms poised on the summit. The
flower bends its head to protect the anthers from rain and so
guard the pollen. These anthers were referred to by botanists of
old as "little hammers of clear gold." The flower is known as the
Scarlet Martagon because of its brilliant scarlet petals and sepals.
Like almost all lilies, there is an underground bulb that stores
nourishment and supplies the flower with food even through the
drought of the desert. The Hebrew name of the lily, *shushan,*
gives its name to instruments of music.

Lily Lilium chalcedonicum   Hebrew: shushan

. . . his lips like lilies, dropping sweet smelling myrrh.

SONG OF SOLOMON 5:13

Locusts

---

*In those days came John the Baptist, preaching
in the wilderness of Judaea, and saying, Repent
ye: for the kingdom of heaven is at hand. . . .
And the same John had his raiment of camel's
hair, and a leathern girdle about his loins; and
his meat was locusts and wild honey. Then went
out to him . . . all Judaea, . . . and were bap-
tized of him in Jordan, confessing their sins.*

MATTHEW 3: 1, 2, 4, 5, 6

The locust is the fruit of the carob tree, and accepted in the East
as the food on which John the Baptist fed; thus it is known there
as St. John's bread. It is native to the eastern Mediterranean region; the Greeks introduced it into their country as well as into
Italy, while the Spaniards carried it into Mexico and South
America, where it is now established. The carob is a sturdy evergreen, growing to fifty feet in height, and is of great beauty. In
the early spring it produces many large clusters of tiny pea-
shaped blossoms; and brown fruits follow in the form of large
thick pods eight inches long. These are filled with a sweet
mucilage that protects the flat bony seeds, and are very nutritious.
In the East this locust fruit is laid on hurdles and dried as food
that is most sustaining for cattle as well as for people. The seeds
are said to be the ancient and original weight used by goldsmiths,
and instituted from early times as carat weight. Each harvest, one
carob tree may carry eight hundred pounds of husks.

Locusts Ceratonia siliqua   Greek: keratiou
. . . and his meat was locusts and wild honey. MATTHEW 3:4

Mallows

---

*But now they that are younger than I have me in
derision, whose fathers I would have disdained to
have set with the dogs of my flock. For want
and famine they were solitary; fleeing into the
wilderness in former time desolate and waste.
Who cut up mallows by the bushes, and juniper
roots for their meat.*   JOB 30: 1, 3, 4

Job cast his mind back to the time when his persecutors and tor-
mentors were of no account or standing. As the patriarch remembered them, they were gathering mallows, which were the sprigs
and leaves of the sea purslane. It is a bush that needs sea air to give
it life, and grows abundantly along the shores of southern Europe
right through to Israel and also on the edges of the Dead Sea. The
original word *malah* signifies "salt," so *malluach* implies a salty-
tasting plant. It can grow as tall as ten feet, and when dried forms
a thick mass of thornless twigs. A tiny purple flower, attached
directly to the stem, blooms in the spring. The leaves are thick
and fleshy, and in spite of their unpleasant taste can be eaten in
times of dire necessity. To this day it is known as the "salt plant,"
and is sometimes eaten by the very poor. There are at least three
other similar species growing in this same area that may also have
shared this history. The Talmud records that Jews working on
the reconstruction of the Temple, in 520–516 B.C., ate these
mallows for food.

Mallows Atriplex halimus   Hebrew: malluach

Who cut up mallows by the bushes . . . JOB 30:4

Mandrake

And when Rachel saw that she bare Jacob no children, Rachel envied her sister. . . . And Reuben went in the days of wheat harvest, and found mandrakes in the field, and brought them unto his mother Leah. Then Rachel said to Leah, Give me, I pray thee, of thy son's mandrakes. . . . And God remembered Rachel. . . . And she conceived, and bare a son . . . and she called his name Joseph. . . .

GENESIS 30: 1, 14, 22, 23, 24

The mandrake belongs to the potato family, Solanaceae. It grows in abundance throughout Syria and nearly all of southern Europe. In early spring a group of leaves shoots out from the root to form a circle flat on the earth. These are large, nearly a foot long and five inches wide in the broadest part, and resemble spinach. The flowers that follow are cup-shaped and borne on a single stem. They are creamy yellow, and heavily veined with purple. The small bright-red fruit is shaped like a tomato and soft and pulpy when cut open. Although it has a peculiar smell, it is much desired and is still generally considered an agreeable delicacy. The mandrake has a large or sometimes enormous root, dark brown and rugged, and resembling the human body in shape. Therefore from early times it has been an object of superstition. The Jews considered the mandrake a certain charm against evil spirits, and others believed that mischief-making elves would find its strange odor unbearable. As indicated in the story of Leah and Rachel, this plant was also thought to induce fertility.

Mandrake Mandragora officinarum   Hebrew: dudaim
And Reuben went in the days of wheat harvest, and found
mandrakes in the field . . .   GENESIS 30:14

Melon (watermelon)

. . . and the children of Israel also wept again,
and said, . . . We remember the fish, which we
did eat in Egypt freely; the cucumbers, and the
melons . . . but now our soul is dried away.
. . . Then Moses heard the people weep
throughout their families, every man in the
door of his tent: and the anger of the Lord was
kindled greatly. . . .   NUMBERS 11:4, 5, 6, 10

This is the only verse in the Bible that mentions these favorite
foods enjoyed by the Israelites in Egypt and longed for as they
traveled through the desert. The watermelon is cultivated along
the banks of the Nile, and is one of the chief foods among the
poorer classes of Egyptians. It thrives so well in that warm and
moist locality that sometimes a single fruit will weigh as much as
thirty pounds. This yellow-flowered trailing plant seems to grow
as easily in dry climates as it does in moist areas. It has a lengthy
leaf deeply gashed into long lobes. The ripe fruit is orange-ruby
color inside; the outer rind is firm and leathery green, speckled
with lemon-colored dots. While it is ripening, the vine is supported by sticks to hold the heavy weight of the melon. Its juicy
pulp is cool and refreshing, and today hundreds of watermelons
may be seen on sale outside the Damascus Gate at Jerusalem. The
Jaffa ones are especially prized.

Melon (watermelon) Citrullus vulgaris   Hebrew: abattichim
We remember . . . the melons . . . NUMBERS 11:5.

Mint

---

*But woe unto you, Pharisees! for ye tithe mint
and rue and all manner of herbs, and pass over
judgment and the love of God: these ought ye
to have done, and not to leave the other undone.*

LUKE 11:42

Only in the New Testament—in Matthew and in Luke—are the
lesser herbs mentioned, and the Jews were entirely scrupulous in
paying the tithe, or tenth, demanded of them. Three varieties of
mint are known to grow in Palestine. They are the garden mint,
the peppermint, and the pennyroyal. The Jews served mint with
their meat dishes, especially at the spring Feast of the Paschal
Lamb. The herb grows wild in ditches and on banks throughout
the Holy Land, and abundantly in Syria, where it covers the hills.
As a plant, it is larger and finer than the usual garden variety. Although it originated in and belongs to the Old World, it is now
very generally cultivated for its valuable medicinal qualities. The
illustration shows a cultivated form of the wild horsemint native
to southern Europe. It has a strong scent. The Greeks called it
mintha, a word later latinized into *mentha*. Pliny gives forty-one
remedies in which mint was thought to be efficacious. The ancient Hebrews, Greeks, and Romans used it, and a writing from
A.D. 37 states that mint was mentioned often in a book of cooking
recipes at that date. The Jews strewed the floors of their synagogues with mint so that its perfume scented the place at each
footfall.

Mint Mentha longifolia

   . . . *for ye pay tithe of mint* . . . MATTHEW 23:23

Mustard

---

*Another parable put he forth unto them, saying,
The kingdom of heaven is like to a grain of mustard seed, which a man took, and sowed in his
field: which indeed is the least of all seeds: but
when it is grown, it is the greatest among herbs,
and becometh a tree, so that the birds of the air
come and lodge in the branches thereof.*

MATTHEW 13:31, 32

The mustard is found growing wild in many parts of the world, including Israel, where it is also cultivated. In that country it grows to so great a size that it can screen a mounted rider, and is a favorite haunt of linnets and finches. During the spring whole plains are yellow with blooming mustard. The flowers are clear lemon yellow, the leaves a rich dark green with a hairy surface. These leaves are used as a vegetable and are regarded as very healthful. Mustard for the table comes from the seeds. The powder ground from them is hot to the taste, and used to flavor meat dishes. It is also used to make poultices or plasters for external application to the body as a cure for some illnesses.

Mustard Brassica nigra   Greek: sinapi

. . . The kingdom of heaven is like to a grain of mustard seed . . .

MATTHEW 13:31

Myrrh (N.T.)

And when they were come into the house, they
saw the young child with Mary his mother, and
fell down, and worshipped him: and when they
had opened their treasures, they presented unto
him gifts; gold, and frankincense, and myrrh.

MATTHEW 2:11

Matthew vividly related the journeyings of the three Wise Men
from the East. The magi brought the infant Jesus precious gifts:
gold for his kingship, frankincense for holiness, and myrrh for
the suffering he must bear while on earth. Myrrh is the gum resin
of a large bush or small tree. The trunk is large and carries
numerous knotted branches, the outer bark of which is thin and
papery. Small leaves grow in clusters on the wood. When the
bark is pierced, a thick white gum appears, which hardens and
turns reddish on exposure to the air. This aromatic gum is
gathered and taken to market, where it has been sold as a spice or
medicine from the earliest times. Myrrh was an ingredient of the
holy anointing oil in the Tabernacle, and of a salve for the
purification of the dead. In Bible days the tree could be found
growing along the coast of the Red Sea in the southern section of
Arabia. The resin was conveyed from the East by traders
mounted on camels. On the night of Christ's crucifixion Nicodemus came *"and brought a mixture of myrrh and aloes, about an*
hundred pound weight. Then took they the body of Jesus, and
wound it in linen clothes with the spices, as the manner of the
Jews is to bury." JOHN 19:39, 40.

Myrrh (N.T.) Commiphora myrrha   Hebrew: mòr
. . . they presented unto him gifts; gold, and frankincense, and myrrh.
MATTHEW 2:11

Myrrh (O.T.)

---

*. . . and, behold, a company of Ishmeelites came
from Gilead with their camels bearing spicery
and balm and myrrh, going to carry it down to
Egypt. And Judah said unto his brethren, What
profit is it if we slay our brother, and conceal his
blood? Come, and let us sell him to the Ishmeelites, and let not our hand be upon him; for he is
our brother and our flesh. And his brethren were
content.*   GENESIS 37:25, 26, 27

One of the best-known stories of the Old Testament concerns the
betrayal of Joseph by his brothers. Later, when in dire need of
food, they visited him at Pharaoh's court and in abject humility
pleaded for his help in obtaining food. In Palestine in the early
spring there thrives amid sand and rock a small shrub, about the
size of a dwarf rhododendron. It grows everywhere—on the
plains and on the sides of mountain ridges, and among the rocks
adjoining the sandy desert of the Arabian peninsula. Throughout
the summer it is a profuse mass of beautiful flowers, shaped like
wild roses and of a rich pink deepening to crimson. Centered
among the five petals are the many stamens of vivid gold and the
single erect pistil. It is the rockrose, and is known as the "lot
plant." The rockrose provides a sweet-smelling gum from all its
parts and the peasants still gather it as they used to do. They use a
small stick wound around with a soft cloth, and on a fine calm
day they carefully wipe the sweet substance from the shrub and
round it into balls. Then it is pressed into cakes and used for perfume. This is the "lot," which through a mistranslation has been
rendered in parts of the Old Testament as "myrrh." The true
myrrh came from the plant called "môr."

Myrrh (o.t.) Cistus creticus   Hebrew: lot

*. . . a company of Ishmeelites came from Gilead with their
camels bearing spicery and balm and myrrh . . .*

GENESIS 37:25

Myrtle

---

*. . . in the second year of Darius, came the word
of the Lord unto Zechariah, the son of Bere-
chiah . . . saying, I saw by night, and behold a
man riding upon a red horse, and he stood among
the myrtle trees that were in the bottom. . . .*

ZECHARIAH 1:7, 8

In a vision the prophet Zechariah saw the angel of the Lord
standing among the myrtle trees. This classical plant was sacred
to Venus, and its name is taken from the Greek word meaning
"perfume." From it were made wreaths to crown the nobility.
Myrtle, prized for its fragrant leaves, is a large evergreen shrub
growing over eighteen feet high. It is abundant in certain localities. The phrase *"the boughs of thick trees"* in LEVITICUS 23:40
refers to the myrtle. Even today the Jews collect it to adorn their
sheds and booths at the Feast of Tabernacles. It bears beautiful
white flowers with a myriad of stamens covering the centers; the
perfume from the blossoms is considered more exquisite than that
of the rose. Purplish-black berries known as mursins have medicinal value. The bark is reddish, and the leaves are oval and very
smooth and shining. This tree was carefully cultivated by the ancient Romans. Today in Italy the leaves are used as a spice, and in
Syria all parts of the plant are dried for perfume. The prophet
Isaiah, comparing the ugly thorns of the brier with the purity of
the myrtle, promised those who were penitent that *"instead of
the brier shall come up the myrtle tree"* ISAIAH 55:13. Its Hebrew
name *hadas* literally means "sweetness"; thus it may be noted in
the book of ESTHER 2:7 that the name was given to a woman:
*"And he brought up Hadassah, that is, Esther, his uncle's
daughter: for she had neither father nor mother, and the maid
was fair and beautiful; whom Mordecai, when her father and
mother were dead, took for his own daughter."*

Myrtle Myrtus communis   Hebrew: hadas

. . . and he stood among the myrtle trees . . . ZECHARIAH 1:8

Nettle

Therefore as I live, saith the Lord of hosts, the God of Israel, Surely Moab shall be as Sodom, and the children of Ammon as Gomorrah, even the breeding of nettles, and saltpits, and a perpetual desolation. . . . ZEPHANIAH 2:9

This nettle-like plant is a strong-growing perennial, with spine-tipped leaves. King Solomon records it as a bush of rapid growth. In the warm country of Palestine, the nettle must have attained great size, for the Bible states that the outcasts were sheltered under it: *"Among the bushes they brayed; under the nettles they were gathered together."* JOB 30:7. Its beautifully formed leaves inspired the designs of the Corinthian capitals in early Greek architecture. The acanthus gave its name to three ancient cities, one of which was in Macedonia: here, as early as the first century before Christ, acanthus-designed coins were fashioned in silver. Today, the plant grows thick and rank in Greece. Its flowers are white streaked with lavender, with a calyx of dark green shaded with purple. The floral spike, standing sixty inches high, can carry twenty-four inches of blossoms.

Nettle Acanthus spinosus   Hebrew: charul

Among the bushes they brayed; under the nettles they were
gathered together.   JOB 30:7

Nuts (walnut)

---

*Who is she that looketh forth as the morning,
fair as the moon, clear as the sun, and terrible
as an army with banners? I went down into the
garden of nuts to see the fruits of the valley,
and to see whether the vine flourished, and the
pomegranates budded.*

SONG OF SOLOMON 6:10, 11

Today most Bible gardens would be called orchards. That of
King Solomon was, in all probability, much more varied and ex-
tensive. One of his most valuable fruit trees was the walnut, a
handsome tree with smooth gray bark and fresh green leaves. It
throws a welcome shade in a hot climate, and as it is fragrant, too,
the tree was a great favorite with the inhabitants of Palestine,
where it grew well in cool locations. In Syria the first long
catkins, which are its flowers, bloom in February, a little before
the leaves unfold. The leaves appear later in March. It bears fruit
in August, the nuts being grouped together in clusters of three or
four. A heavy green rind encasing the actual nut is steeped in
boiling water to produce a good rich brown dye. In Jesus' time,
walnut trees grew on the shores of the Sea of Galilee. His coat,
which was without seam, is thought to have been a rich brown,
and the dye is said to have been made from the leaves and nuts of
the walnut tree. It was known to the Greeks as the Persian tree:
they held their feasts under the shadow of its branches. In heathen mythology it was dedicated to the god Jove.

Nuts (walnut) Juglans regia   Hebrew: egoz

I went down into the garden of nuts . . . SONG OF SOLOMON 6:11

Nuts (pistachio)

And their father Israel said unto them, If it must be so now, do this; take of the best fruits in the land in your vessels, and carry down the man a present, a little balm, and a little honey, spices, and myrrh, nuts, and almonds.

GENESIS 43:11

Jacob's sons carried pistachio nuts to Egypt. The tree was once peculiar to Syria, and one of its governors, Lucius Vitellus, first introduced it into Europe during the reign of Tiberius. Since that time, it has spread over the shores of the Mediterranean as far west as Spain, and is very common in Israel. Today the sloping hills in the south of Italy are covered by beautiful orchards which include the pistachio tree. It grows to a height of twenty to thirty feet. The bark of the trunk is russet, the younger branches are light brown, and the gray-green leaves are winged. The latter, when bruised, smell like the fruit. From the branches grow loose clusters of flowers; when these wither, the nuts form. These are oval, and have a double shell: the outer one is thin, dry, and red; the inner kernel is pale green, and has a very agreeable oily, sweet taste. In Europe they are eaten as a confection.

Nuts (pistachio) Pistacia vera   Hebrew: botnim
. . . and carry down the man a present, a little balm, and a little
honey, spices, and myrrh, nuts, and almonds . . . GENESIS 43:11

Oak (holly oak)

So Jacob came to Luz, which is in the land of Canaan, that is, Beth-el, he and all the people that were with him. And he built there an altar, and called the place El-beth-el: because there God appeared unto him, when he fled from the face of his brother. But Deborah Rebekah's nurse died, and she was buried beneath Beth-el under an oak: and the name of it was called Allon-bachuth. GENESIS 35:6, 7, 8

This is the holly oak or holm tree, mentioned also in the apocryphal History of Susanna. The word "holly" was originally spelled "holy." It applied to the small bush holly as well. This holly oak is a magnificent tree, reaching a height of fifty feet. The three-inch leaves resemble those of holly, as their edges are armed with spines; they have a convex surface, and are rich shiny green, with lighter undersides. As the young shoots grow bigger they lose their gray feltlike covering. The fruit is an acorn, three quarters of an inch long. It is held in a yellow-green cup, covered with slender scales. Since the roots of this oak descend to a great depth, it is to be found on firm dry ground, and never in swampy soil. Pliny mentions some holm oaks growing in his day as being fifteen hundred years old. He also states that one tree in the Vatican gardens was said to be older than Rome itself. The holm oak is a tree that prefers to grow alone, and never in forests; also, it grows well near the sea. It is native to the Mediterranean region, and is found frequently throughout Europe. In all mythologies the oak has stood for strength and long life. It was sacred to the gods Thor and Jove, and under its shadow sacrifices have been offered and kings have been crowned.

Oak (holly oak) Quercus ilex   Hebrew: allon

. . . and she was buried beneath Beth-el under an oak . . .

GENESIS 35:8

Oak (Valonia oak)

Open thy doors, O Lebanon, that the fire may devour thy cedars. Howl, fir tree; for the cedar is fallen; because the mighty are spoiled: howl, O ye oaks of Bashan; for the forest of the vintage is come down. There is a voice of the howling of the shepherds; for their glory is spoiled: a voice of the roaring of young lions; for the pride of Jordan is spoiled.   ZECHARIAH 11:1, 2, 3

Zechariah's prophecies were couched in symbols, among which was the oak. As many as six species of oak are to be found in Israel. The Valonia oak here discussed sheds its leaves every autumn. These leaves are nearly four inches long, and in shape resemble those of the European oak, *Quercus robur*. The tree grows to the same handsome proportions as the European variety. In the autumn it changes its color to a sienna copper tone. The acorn it bears is very large and that, too, becomes reddish orange, its tan cup covered with long flat strips resembling suede leather. An insect attacks the bark of the tree and this results in galls or swellings, that contain allic acid and tannin from which writing ink is made. A strong black dye of commercial value is derived from the acorn cups. Swine are fed acorns, and in Algeria and Greece the poor eat them too. Bashan, meaning "rich and fruitful," is a rich hilly district. In the Bible it is celebrated for its fertile valleys, and for hills covered with forests of these Valonia oaks. The word Valonia comes from the Greek word meaning "acorn."

Oak (Valonia oak) Quercus aegilops   Hebrew: allon
He heweth him down cedars, and taketh the cypress and the oak . . .

ISAIAH 44:14

Oil Tree

---

*I will open rivers in high places, and fountains
in the midst of the valleys: I will make the
wilderness a pool of water, and the dry land
springs of water. I will plant in the wilderness
the cedar, the shittah tree, and the myrtle, and
the oil tree . . . that they may see, and know,
and consider, and understand together, that the
hand of the Lord hath done this, and the Holy
One of Israel hath created it.*

ISAIAH 41:18, 19, 20

The oil tree is native to the Levant, and also grows in Iran and
Siberia. It is most common in the Caucasus, and in Circassia on
the banks of the river Terek. This tree reaches a height of fifteen
to twenty feet. Its lanceolate leaves are rich green, with light un-
dersurface, and are hairy all over. They are two to three inches
long and joined to the branch by short petioles. Its reddish-brown
fruit resembles an olive. Since *shemen* means oil, it can be as-
sumed that the tree so referred to was an oil-producing one. If it
is trimmed when young it can be kept low as a hedge plant. Other
regional names for it are "Jerusalem willow," because of its leaf
shape and general habit of growth; the French *chalef*, an adapta-
tion from the Arabic *khalef* for willow; the Persian *kalaf*; the
Arabic *zackum*. It releases a deep yellow gum used in treating eye
ailments.

Oil Tree Elaeagnus angustifolia   Hebrew: etz shemen
I will plant in the wilderness the cedar, the shittah tree, and the
myrtle, and the oil tree . . .   ISAIAH 41:19

Olive

And it came to pass at the end of forty days, that Noah opened the window of the ark which he had made. . . . And he stayed yet other seven days; and again he sent forth the dove out of the ark; and the dove came in to him in the evening; and, lo, in her mouth was an olive leaf pluckt off: so Noah knew that the waters were abated from off the earth. GENESIS 8:6, 10, 11

The waters must have risen gently and departed quickly, not to have spoiled the trees. Oliveyards were very numerous in Palestine, the olive becoming the most important tree cultivated in that area. One tree could supply a whole family with fats, for olive oil was used instead of butter. However, if neglected, the olive ceases to bear fruit; it must be situated near the sea to flourish. The flowers of pale yellow with deeper yellow centers are small but enlarge as they open. The leaves of this evergreen are gray-green, long, slender, and of shimmering beauty: *"His branches shall spread, and his beauty shall be as the olive tree. . . ."* HOSEA 14:6. The unripened green fruit is about an inch long, and is eaten with coarse brown bread. Harvest time is in October, when long poles are used to beat the olives down from the branches. These olives, which turn black when ripe, are gathered into baskets, then crushed by a large upright wheel made of stone, the oil thus obtained being carried off through a spout into a sunken vat. Small quantities are pounded separately in a mortar to prepare the oil for the lamps of the Temple. *"And thou shalt command the children of Israel, that they bring thee pure oil olive beaten for the light, to cause the lamp to burn always."* EXODUS 27:20. A full-sized tree yields a half ton of oil yearly. It is the most frequently mentioned tree in the Roman classics. Jesus spent the night before his crucifixion in the Garden of Gethsemane, which translated means "garden with the olive press."

Olive Olea europaea   Hebrew: zayit

Thou shalt have olive trees throughout all thy coasts . . .

DEUTERONOMY 28:40

Onion

---

*We remember the fish, which we did eat in
Egypt . . . the leeks, and the onions . . . but
now our soul is dried away: there is nothing at
all, beside this manna, before our eyes.*

NUMBERS 11:5, 6

This is the only mention of the onion in the Bible, despite its universal use as a food throughout biblical times. The vegetable grows very much larger in warm dry countries than in temperate places. Its flavor is sweet and inviting, and the Palestinian onion has no equal anywhere. It probably originated in Persia, though it has been cultivated in Egypt from time immemorial, and representations of the onion can be seen carved on the excavated tombs. Herodotus says that when the Great Pyramid of Khufu was erected, a huge amount of money was spent in supplying the builders with onions. To some Egyptian priests the vegetable symbolized the universe, for they saw in the round globe of the onion the spheres of heaven, earth, and hell. This type of onion grows beneath the soil, but sends up a long inflated stem that terminates in a ball-shaped cluster of tiny white flowerets, each with six tepals. The fresh young leaves are long and tubular. Ancient medical lists include twenty-six remedies that mention the onion.

Onion Allium cepa   Hebrew: betsel

We remember . . . the cucumbers, and the melons, and the leeks,
and the onions . . .   NUMBERS 11:5

Onycha

---

*And the Lord said unto Moses, Take unto thee
sweet spices, stacte, and onycha, and galbanum;
these sweet spices with pure frankincense: of
each shall there be a like weight: and thou shalt
make it a perfume, a confection after the art of
the apothecary, tempered together, pure and
holy: and thou shalt beat some of it very small,
and put of it before the testimony in the tabernacle of the congregation, where I will meet
with thee: it shall be unto you most holy.*

EXODUS 30:34, 35, 36

The onycha referred to is a rockrose, and produces the gum
known as labdanum. Onycha blossoms are fully three inches
across, are white, and have at the base of each petal a blotch of
glowing scarlet-rose deepening to black. A gold center is made up
of a hundred small stamens and a pistil. Onycha in Greek means
"fingernail," and the markings on the petals probably gave rise to
the name. The bush is three feet tall, and all through the long dry
season it is a mass of blooms. Its leaves are dark sage green, finely
veined and strongly scented. Late in the year a soft glutinous
resin, highly aromatic and fragrant, exudes from these leaves and
stems. The Orientals credit it with great medicinal qualities, and
it was highly regarded in biblical times. According to Dioscorides, the resin of this plant was first noticed long ago because
of a herd of goats: the animals, after browsing among the young
shoots of onycha, would return home with their long beards
coated with the sticky substance, which hardened in the air.

Onycha Cistus ladaniferus   Hebrew: shecheleth
. . . I yielded a pleasant odour like . . . onyx . . . ECCLESIASTICUS 24:15

Palm

And they removed from Marah, and came unto Elim: and in Elim were twelve fountains of water, and threescore and ten palm trees; and they pitched there. And they removed from Elim, and encamped by the Red Sea.

NUMBERS 33:9, 10

Elim was one of the oases where the Israelites made camp during their journey to the Promised Land. Many naturalists from Herodotus to Linnaeus have agreed that the palm is the most remarkable of all trees. When fully grown the date palm is as high as a hundred feet, its shape quite distinctive and beautiful. One single upright trunk rises from the ground to the topmost leaves. It has no branches, but grows compound leaves six feet in length and arranged like a coronet atop the rugged trunk. The fruit of this palm is the date, which hangs in clusters below the leaves. It is a most nutritious food for the Arabs and their camels. Mats are woven from the leaves, while the fibers provide thread and rigging for boats. There is sap in the palm tree which, after fermentation, is used as a liquor. It grows everywhere in the Holy Land and attains a great age. Jericho was known as the city of palm trees and Phoenicia as the "Land of Palms." According to the New Testament, palm fronds were carried by the crowd when they went to meet Jesus, crying "Hosanna" JOHN 12:13. He had left Bethany, which means "the house of dates," to enter Jerusalem. There is also the verse, "*After this I beheld, and lo, a great multitude, which no man could number, . . . stood before the throne, . . . clothed with white robes, and palms in their hands . . .*" REVELATION 7:9.

Palm Phoenix dactylifera   Hebrew: tamar

. . . and brought them to Jericho, the city of palm trees . . .

II CHRONICLES 28:15

Pannag (millet)

Judah, and the land of Israel, they were thy merchants: they traded in thy market wheat of Minnith, and pannag, and honey, and oil, and balm.   EZEKIEL 27:17

These words told of grain foods sold to the Ammonites. Minnith was their town in the time of Jephthah, and it lay four miles east of Heshbon, famous for its wheat. Pannag is a millet, and has a head heavy with vast numbers of edible seeds. The related Latin word *panis* means bread. Since pannag seeds are hard and very white, they make good flour. Ezekiel received an order from the Lord God to make bread, and mix together wheat, barley, beans, lentils, and pannag. The mixture was moistened with camel's milk, oil, or butter. It was the main food that the common people ate. Ezekiel, too, was forced to rely on this unpalatable fare throughout the time of siege and famine (EZEKIEL 4:9). The name "dochan" is given to the pannag because of its amazing fruitfulness, for one stalk can carry a thousand grains. It is the "Turkish millet," and in Spain, Italy, and the rest of southern Europe, is cultivated extensively for food to take the place of oats and barley.

Pannag (millet) Panicum miliaceum   Hebrew: dochan

. . . they traded in thy market wheat of Minnith, and pannag . . .

EZEKIEL 27:17

Pine Tree

---

*The glory of Lebanon shall come unto thee, the
fir tree, the pine tree, and the box together, to
beautify the place of my sanctuary. . . .*

ISAIAH 60:13

The "pine" here mentioned is the handsome Cilician fir. It grows
very tall, and is a striking representative of the fir family. Its
gray-green needles flash like silver in the sunlight. Pines take their
name from the Latin *pinus*, a raft, as the wood was easy to cut
and was used by men of primitive tribes and races for boats and
rafts. When the cone of this "pine" is cut lengthwise, the mark
on its surface resembles the form of a hand. According to legend,
this is the hand of Christ, a mark of his blessing on the tree that
sheltered Mary, his mother, when she and her family were in
flight from Herod's soldiers.

Pine Tree Abies cilicica   Hebrew: tidhar

The glory of Lebanon shall come unto thee, the fir tree, the pine tree . . .   ISAIAH 60:13

Pomegranate

And Saul tarried in the uttermost part of Gibeah under a pomegranate tree which is in Migron. . . .   I SAMUEL 14:2

Jonathan's brilliant exploit in Michmash is described in this Old Testament story. "Pomegranate" literally means "apple with grains," the reference being to the many clear ruby-colored seeds, covered with a thin skin and full of juice, found in each fruit. It is a very refreshing delicacy to the dwellers in a hot and thirsty land. This plant which grows wild in Iran and Syria, is a low shrub or a small tree, with a straight stem, reddish bark, and many spreading branches. The lance-shaped leaves are dark green and highly polished, the firm and waxlike blossoms bright coral red, and the delicate silky and crinkled petals quite fiery in their brilliance. When the fruit is ripe it is the size of an orange, maroon in color, with a thick jacket enveloping the pulp and crowded seeds. A syrup made from the seeds is known as grenadine. The first sherbet was a preparation of pomegranate juice mixed with snow. Apothecaries use the blossoms, known as balausts, in the preparation of an astringent medicine used in treating dysentery. The plant is also known as *malum granatum*, and in French *pomme granate*. The silver shekel of Jerusalem, in circulation from 143 to 135 B.C., bears engravings of three pomegranates. Hiram of Tyre used the pomegranate as a model when he was building Solomon's Temple: "*And he made the pillars, and two rows round about upon the one network, to cover the chapiters that were upon the top, with pomegranates. . . . And the chapiters upon the two pillars had pomegranates also above, over against the belly which was by the network: and the pomegranates were two hundred in rows round about upon the other chapiter*" I KINGS 7:18, 20. The ephod of the high priest was bordered at the hem with pomegranates (EXODUS 28:31, 33, 34).

(152)

Pomegranate Punica granatum   Hebrew: rimmon

And Saul tarried . . . under a pomegranate tree . . . I SAMUEL 14:2

Poplar

And Jacob took him rods of green poplar, and of the hazel and chesnut tree; and pilled white strakes in them, and made the white appear which was in the rods. And he set the rods which he had pilled before the flocks in the gutters in the watering troughs when the flocks came to drink, that they should conceive when they came to drink. And the flocks conceived before the rods, and brought forth cattle ring-straked, speckled, and spotted.

GENESIS 30:37, 38, 39

The poplar here referred to is found in the hills of Israel, where it grows to between thirty and sixty feet tall. It also thrives in wet places in Syria. HOSEA 4:13 records: *"They sacrifice upon the tops of the mountains, and burn incense upon the hills, under oaks and poplars and elms, because the shadow thereof is good. . . ."* It is fast-growing, especially when young, and produces long straight shoots and green leaves backed with white. The flowers, in the form of catkins, appear before the leaves, and the buds are covered with a resinous varnish. They give out a balsamic odor when burned.

Poplar Populus alba   Hebrew: libneh
And Jacob took him rods of green poplar . . . GENESIS 30:37

Reed

Behold now behemoth, which I made with thee;
he eateth grass as an ox. . . . Surely the moun-
tains bring him forth food, where all the beasts
of the field play. He lieth under the shady trees,
in the covert of the reed, and fens. The shady
trees cover him with their shadow; the willows
of the brook compass him about.

JOB 40: 15, 20, 21, 22

Behemoth was a huge amphibious animal, probably the hippopotamus or river horse. It was large, powerful, and unwieldy, living in the water but coming on shore to feed on green herbs, grass, grain, and branches of trees. The Hebrew word *agmon* signifies a hollow stalk that would hold water like a pipe. Another literal rendering is "flowing together like water," and this is descriptive of the habitat of this reed. The Latin word *arundo* also means reed, and is applied to the *Arundo donax*, found in Israel. *Aghanim* is modern Arabic for the common marsh reed growing by the sides of rivers and in standing waters. This reed of Egypt and Israel is very tall—the cane grows twelve feet high —and carries at the top a magnificent head of blossom, very dense and silky. It is so large and beautiful that it resembles a plume, purple in color, and having a lustrous sheen. Many country people of Asia use it to decorate their houses. "The taller the reed, the lower it bends" is a saying that is true of the *Phragmites*, since it stands high in clumps. Its roots hold fast in the mud of the river bank; thus the noise is quite noticeable when the wind sweeps through the leaves, causing the blossom heads almost to touch the water. Pens for writing on parchment were cut and fashioned from this reed, and the stems were used as a linear measuring device. "*And he brought me thither, and, behold, there was a man, whose appearance was like the appearance of brass, with a line of flax in his hand, and a measuring reed; and he stood in the gate.*" EZEKIEL 40: 3.

Reed Phragmites communis   Hebrew: agmon

He lieth under the shady trees, in the covert of the reed, and fens.

JOB 40:21

Rie (spelt)

So there was hail, and fire mingled with the hail,
very grievous, . . . and the hail smote every
herb of the field. . . . But the wheat and the
rie were not smitten: for they were not grown
up. And Moses went out of the city from Phar-
aoh, and spread abroad his hands unto the Lord:
and the thunders . . . ceased. . . .

EXODUS 9:24, 25, 32, 33

Here is another part of the story of the seven plagues sent by the
Lord upon the land of Pharaoh to punish him for his hardness of
heart in keeping the children of Israel captive. What we know as
rye is a cereal grain not native to Egypt. It came from the lands
farther north and was grown only in small quantities. Biblical
"rie" was probably spelt. Its stalk is taller than that of wheat and
it will grow in soil too poor even for grass to thrive. Bread made
from spelt is far inferior to the cakes of flour baked from wheat,
but it will yield a crop from the soil not rich enough to grow
wheat. That it was a useful grain and grown by the people can be
judged by reading the words of ISAIAH 28:24, 25 26: "*Doth the*
plowman plow all day to sow? doth he open and break the clods
of his ground? When he hath made plain the face thereof, doth
he not cast . . . in the principal wheat and the appointed barley
and the rie in their place? For his God doth instruct him to dis-
cretion, and doth teach him." Grain was threshed by the staff or
the flail or by an instrument with teeth that was drawn over the
sheaves by oxen. When the grain was loosened, the whole heap
was thrown with a fork against the wind to blow away the chaff.
Then the grain was sifted and ground into flour. The mill
consisted of two circular stones, each six inches thick and
twenty-four inches across. The grain was poured through a hole
in the upper stone, which was rotated by a handle, the crushed
meal then being squeezed out around the edges and received into
a cloth.

Rie (spelt) Triticum aestivum var. spelta   Hebrew: kussemeth
But the wheat and the rie were not smitten . . . EXODUS 9:32
The above illustration shows both barley and rie. The rie is on the left.

Rolling Thing
(rose of Jericho)

The nations shall rush like the rushing of many waters: but God shall rebuke them, and they shall flee far off, and shall be chased as the chaff of the mountains before the wind, and like a rolling thing before the whirlwind. ISAIAH 17:13

The "rolling thing" is a plant that looks like a dry withered ball when it is found lying on the fiercely hot sands of the barren plains surrounding the Dead Sea. It is also known as the resurrection flower and as the rose of Jericho because the dried-up ball, blown about over large areas as a "rolling thing," will at last come to rest and, with the help of a little moisture, take root again. Then its dried stems unroll. Tiny flowers and fresh green leaves appear on them; the whole plant opens flat upon the ground. It is found in Egypt, and pilgrims in Israel seek the ball as a holy relic. The early Christians considered it sacred. This dried-up plant with its power to bloom again after appearing dead was to them a symbol of Christian immortality; hence they named it "the holy resurrection flower."

Rolling Thing (rose of Jericho) Anastatica hierochuntica Hebrew: gulgal
. . . *like a rolling thing before the whirlwind.* ISAIAH 17:13

Rose (narcissus)

The wilderness and the solitary place shall be glad for them; and the desert shall rejoice, and blossom as the rose. It shall blossom abundantly, and rejoice even with joy and singing: the glory of Lebanon shall be given unto it, the excellency of Carmel and Sharon, they shall see the glory of the Lord, and the excellency of our God.

ISAIAH 35:1, 2

In this instance the Hebrew word translated "rose" indicates a plant with a bulbous root, so it cannot apply to a true rosebush. The accepted opinion is that the little flower alluded to is the yellow *Narcissus tazetta*. The earliest Chaldean paraphrase of the Bible gives the Hebrew word *narkom*, meaning narcissus, and the Talmud also refers to it as *narkom*. The Iraneans call it *norgus*, which throughout the East has signified the polyanthus narcissus. In Israel this narcissus is a dazzling golden yellow, a color not seen in cooler climates. It grows wild in the desert from the Mediterranean Sea to the center of Israel, near Jaffa, and in January the land is a profusion of color. "Tazetta," derived from the Italian word *tazza*, meaning "a cup," refers to the central crown or corona.

Rose (narcissus) Narcissus tazetta   Hebrew: chabazeleth

. . . *the desert shall rejoice, and blossom as the rose.* ISAIAH 35:1

Rose of Sharon

---

*I am the rose of Sharon, and the lily of the val-
leys. As the lily among thorns, so is my love
among the daughters.*   SONG OF SOLOMON 2:1, 2

The literal translation of the Hebrew word *chabazeleth* would indicate that the "rose" of Sharon was not a shrub or vine of the
genus *Rosa*, but rather a bulb-growing plant. Botanists have established it as most likely a tulip, *Tulipa sharonensis*, or Sharon
tulip. The plant is ten inches high, with silver gray-green leaves
and glowing red flowers. In Turkey the tulip is known as *shul-
iban*, or turban, from the similarity of the shape of the flower to
that headdress. The Sharon tulip is native to, and grows in
profusion on, the plain of Sharon, which is situated between Carmel and Jaffa and is about sixty miles long. After the annual
spring rains the view from the plain is one of surpassing richness
and beauty, with the lowering hills of Judah on the east facing
the shining waters of the Mediterranean on the west. Most of the
land is laid out in crops, while the uncultivated parts of the plain
are covered in spring and early summer with a wealth of flowers
including this one. A favorite old hymn refers to Jesus as a "rose
of Sharon."

Rose of Sharon Tulipa sharonensis   Hebrew: chabazeleth

I am the rose of Sharon . . . SONG OF SOLOMON 2:1

Rue

---

*But woe unto you, Pharisees! for ye tithe mint
and rue and all manner of herbs, and pass over
judgment and the love of God: these ought ye
to have done, and not to leave the other undone.
Woe unto you, Pharisees! for ye love the upper-
most seats in the synagogues, and greetings in
the markets.* LUKE 11:42, 43

The rue, only this once mentioned in the Bible, is a garden herb,
and very valuable to man. There are four varieties grown, the
most common being the species named here. The specific name,
graveolens, means "strong smelling." Rue was gathered for use as
a disinfectant, and scattered in courts of justice to protect officials
from the terrible prison fever and stenches prevailing in olden
times. It was highly prized by the ancients, for they liked its peculiar, though very strong, taste. Pliny mentions honeyed wine
flavored with rue, as well as eighty-four remedies containing rue.
In the Holy Land the plant grows five feet tall. Its flowers form
clusters atop upright stems, each flower having four petals col-
ored a sharp lemon-yellow and surrounding a little dome of
green in the center. As a perennial it is a welcome addition in gardens for its strong habit of growth and for its usefulness in
cookery and medicine.

Rue Ruta graveolens.   Greek: peganon

  . . . for ye tithe mint and rue and all manner of herbs . . . LUKE 11:42

Rush

(For we are but of yesterday, and know nothing, because our days upon earth are a shadow:) Shall not they teach thee, and tell thee, and utter words out of their heart? Can the rush grow up without mire? can the flag grow without water? Whilst it is yet in his greenness, and not cut down, it withereth before any other herb. So are the paths of all that forget God; and the hypocrite's hope shall perish. JOB 8:9, 10, 11, 12, 13

Twenty varieties of this luxuriant and grasslike plant inhabit streams and edges of rivers in Israel. This one, *Juncus effusus*, is over four feet high. It is known as the common soft or bog rush, and is found in wet places where it is useful in binding the soil beneath the water. Each separate part of the dark flowers is set in a plaited manner, and the entire cluster bends and has a drooping habit. The whiplike cylindrical leaves have for centuries been cut and utilized in basketry. Rushes are also used to make mats, shallow panniers to hold grapes, snares for game, chair seats, and other household articles. Isaiah speaks of them, saying: *"And the parched ground shall become a pool, and the thirsty land springs of water: in the habitation of dragons, where each lay, shall be grass with reeds and rushes."* ISAIAH 35:7.

Rush Juncus effusus   Hebrew: agmon

Can the rush grow up without mire? . . . JOB 8:11

Saffron

---

*Thy plants are an orchard of pomegranates, with
pleasant fruits; camphire, with spikenard . . .
and saffron; calamus and cinnamon, with all trees
of frankincense; myrrh and aloes, with all the
chief spices: A fountain of gardens, a well of
living waters, and streams from Lebanon. Awake,
O north wind; and come, thou south; blow upon
my garden, that the spices thereof may flow
out. . . .* SONG OF SOLOMON 4:13, 14, 15, 16

In biblical times the saffron was very important to the people of
the East as a condiment and sweet perfume, the stigmas being
particularly valued for their food-coloring property. These
stigmas are a vivid orange, are dry, narrow, and threadlike, and
emit a peculiar and aromatic odor. They taste bitter, and stain the
lips. Packed tightly together, they are sold as cake saffron, and in
this form are conveyed from Iran into India, where they are used
to add yellow shades to the curry. The flower grows from a bulb
and blooms in the autumn. It is a clear lavender and has a delicate
scent. Homer and Theophrastus mention it in their writings, and
Pliny records that the benches of the public theaters were strewn
with saffron, and the costly petals were also placed in small
fountains, to diffuse the scent into public halls. In Europe it is
used as a flavoring and as a coloring ingredient, and druggists add
it to medicines. One grain of commercial saffron contains the
stigmas of nine flowers; some four thousand blossoms are required
to make an ounce.

Saffron Crocus sativus   Hebrew: karkom

Spikenard and saffron; calamus and cinnamon, with all trees
of frankincense . . .   SONG OF SOLOMON 4:14

Scarlet

. . . then the priest shall pronounce the house clean, because the plague is healed. And he shall take to cleanse the house two birds, and cedar wood, and scarlet, and hyssop: . . . and he shall take the cedar wood, and the hyssop, and the scarlet, and the living bird, and dip them in the blood of the slain bird, and in the running water, and sprinkle the house seven times. . . .

LEVITICUS 14:48, 49, 51

Thus was the purification of a dwelling house performed by the priests after a season of plague. The oak from which the scarlet of the Old Testament was derived is a large evergreen shrub, growing ten to twenty feet high and having a sturdy, dense, and neat habit. Its leaves are small, very spiny and thorny, and the whole plant resembles a holly tree. Acorns over half an inch long form in the autumn, the cups half covered with spreading spiny scales. This oak is native to the Mediterranean region from Spain to Syria. Its young shoots are covered with white, soft down which is the breeding ground of the kermes insect, *Chermes ilicis.* These creatures yield a beautiful scarlet dye remarkable for its richness and lasting quality. The scarlet was known commercially as "grain" and "scarlet grain," and later as the "grain tree." When the bark of this kermes oak is steeped in boiling water, it yields a black dye, once used to dye hair.

Scarlet Quercus coccifera   Hebrew: shani
And he shall take the cedar wood, and the hyssop, and the scarlet . . .
                                                              LEVITICUS 14:51

Shittah Tree

. . . I will make the wilderness a pool of water,
and the dry land springs of water. I will plant in
the wilderness the cedar, the shittah tree, and
the myrtle, and the oil tree; I will set in the des-
ert the fir tree, and the pine, and the box tree to-
gether: That they may see, and know, and
consider, and understand together, that the hand
of the Lord hath done this. . . .

ISAIAH 41:18, 19, 20

The shittah tree is mentioned in the Bible only once, but its wood is referred to many times as *shittim*, which is the plural form of *shittah* in Hebrew. It is an acacia, one of the thorny trees of the Holy Land, and very sweet-smelling, with yellow flowers and soft green leaves. The shittah tree was abundant in Egypt, and existed in limited quantities even in the deserts of Arabia. It is as large as a mulberry tree, and has a gnarled rough black bark and angular spreading branches, covered with sharp thorns. "*And the Lord spake unto Moses, saying, Speak unto the children of Is-rael. . . . And they shall make an ark of shittim wood: two cubits and a half shall be the length thereof, and a cubit and a half the breadth thereof, and a cubit and a half the height thereof. And thou shalt overlay it with pure gold. . . .*" EXODUS 25:1, 2, 10, 11. This ark, ten feet in length, was the first piece of sacred furniture fashioned for the Tabernacle. The shittim wood is or-ange and very beautiful, close grained, and very heavy. It darkens with age, and is not attacked by insects. This tree grows as a tor-rent tree, thriving in the wadies of Sinai and the Dead Sea, but is not found in upper Israel, though the book of NUMBERS (33:49) records that the Israelites, after a long march, pitched their tents by Jordan, "*from Beth-jesimoth even unto Abel-shittim.*" "Abel-shittim" is translated "meadow of the acacias." The tree grows also in northeast Africa, and produces gum arabic and gum senegal.

Shittah Tree Acacia seyal   Hebrew: shittah
I will plant in the wilderness . . . the shittah tree . . . ISAIAH 41:19

Spices

And when the queen of Sheba heard of the fame
of Solomon, she came to prove Solomon with
hard questions at Jerusalem, with a very great
company, and camels that bare spices, and gold
in abundance, and precious stones. . . . And she
said to the king, It was a true report which I
heard in mine own land of thine acts, and of thy
wisdom.   II CHRONICLES 9: 1, 5

These spices were used for the holy incense in the Tabernacle. In
the English Bibles the word for the astragal plant is inaccurately
translated "spices." Its product is not properly a spice. It is the
gum tragacanth of commerce, and the plant is known as wild
tragacanth or thorny astragal, the *necoth* of the Bible. In spite of
its pretty pea-like blossoms of pale yellow, it is a formidable little
shrub. The desert astragal, as it is also known, is native to Israel,
thriving as well on the desert sands as in the cooler lands of the
north where the rainfall is heavier. One finds it on the shores of
the Dead Sea, 1,292 feet below sea level. Yet again, it is at the
summit of Mount Hermon, 9,232 feet above sea level. An astragal
—there are over twenty varieties—can be a ball made up of hundreds of spikes and only two feet in height, or a tall shrub, barbed
and resistant to humans and beasts. The biblical species is dwarf
and woody with long pinnate leaves and strong prickly thorns.
The whole plant is fenced about with spines, sharp as needles.
From the thorns a precious resin exudes during hours of sunshine.
A ball of cotton is rubbed over the plant to collect the accumulated lumps of gum.

Spices Astragalus tragacantha   Hebrew: besem

. . . and camels that bare spices . . . II CHRONICLES 9: I

Spikenard

And being in Bethany in the house of Simon the leper, as he sat at meat, there came a woman having an alabaster box of ointment of spikenard very precious; and she brake the box, and poured it on his head. And there were some that had indignation within themselves, and said, Why was this waste of the ointment made? For it might have been sold for more than three hundred pence, and have been given to the poor. And they murmured against her. And Jesus said, Let her alone; why trouble ye her? she hath wrought a good work on me. MARK 14:3, 4, 5, 6

Spikenard is native to Nepal, Bhutan, and the valleys of Tibet. The Indian word for the plant is *tamul*, meaning an herb with a most agreeable perfume. King Solomon rejoiced in it: "*While the king sitteth at his table, my spikenard sendeth forth the smell thereof.*" SONG OF SOLOMON 1:12. Its Latin name *Nardostachys*, meaning "ear of wheat," refers to the shape of the flowerets, and the Indian name *jatamansi* relates to the shaggy hair, or "ermine tails," covering the stems. In ancient times the fragrant ointment from this small herbaceous plant was exported in large amounts. It was known as "sinbul Hindi" or "Indian spike." The Romans used it for anointing the head. It is a rich rose red and very sweetly scented. In the spring upright spikes grow from the roots and carry little groups of pink flowers at their tops. From the lower hairy stems comes the exquisite perfume obtained by the simple method of tying them together by the roots. So expensive was the perfume after its long journey from northern India to Palestine, that one pound of it cost three hundred denarii. The denarius was the equivalent of a laborer's daily wage. Today, as in biblical times, the spikenard is carried on camelback in alabaster boxes that preserve the essential perfume.

(178)

Spikenard Nardostachys jatamansi   Hebrew: nard   Greek: narkom
. . . an alabaster box of ointment of spikenard very precious . . .

MARK 14:3

Stacte (storax)

And the Lord said unto Moses, Take unto thee sweet spices, stacte, and onycha, and galbanum; these sweet spices with pure frankincense: of each shall there be a like weight: and thou shalt make it a perfume, a confection after the art of the apothecary, tempered together, pure and holy.   EXODUS 30:34, 35

Stacte is a gum that exudes from certain trees, and was a component of the perfume to be offered in the Holy Place. The Hebrew word *nataph* means literally "a liquid drop." This stacte or storax is a beautiful shrub that reaches the height of a good-sized tree when well-grown. It is abundant on the lower hills of Israel. In March the blossoms appear in clusters of four or five together, beautifully perfumed. The flowers resemble a snowdrop in shape, and are pure waxen white with vivid orange anthers protruding from the center. When in full bloom, the bush looks as though it is covered with a light fall of snow. The leaves are clear shining green on the upper surface, and gray-white underneath. Incisions are made in the branches so that a resin will flow out in a liquid state. This is then gathered in reeds, a practice that has given the resin the name of "storax kalamites." After it has hardened, the stacte is scraped off in irregular compact masses, interspersed with smaller drops known as "tears." These contain resin and benzoic acid and will dissolve in wine. In early days in England, storax was used to perfume pomades. Today the Roman Catholic Church uses it in incense.

Stacte (storax) Styrax officinalis   Hebrew: nataph
And the Lord said unto Moses, Take unto thee sweet spices, stacte,
and onycha, and galbanum . . .   EXODUS 30:34

Strange Vine

Yet I had planted thee a noble vine, wholly a right seed: how then art thou turned into the degenerate plant of a strange vine unto me?

JEREMIAH 2:21

This strange vine is a bushy and sometimes a climbing deciduous shrub, with smooth and slightly ribbed shoots. The many leaflets are ovate or diamond-shaped, with serrated edges, and joined on the stalk in multiples of threes. Each leaflet, which is a darker green on the upper surface, has a paler gray-green underside, and is very smooth. The flowers are borne in long-stalked cymes, ripening later into round fruit a quarter of an inch in diameter and somewhat the shape of a spinning top. This fruit is bright red and looks like a cluster of red currants. The vine is native to Turkey and Syria. It is prolific in the mountains of Israel, and grows even on those as high as five thousand feet. It is a handsome plant, and is free from the pests that destroy the beauty of many shrubs in hot desert country. It is not of use to man as an edible fruit.

Strange Vine Vitis orientalis   Hebrew: gephen nochriah
. . . *the degenerate plant of a strange vine* . . . JEREMIAH 2:21

Sweet Cane (sugar cane)

. . . I have not caused thee to serve with an offering, nor wearied thee with incense. Thou hast bought me no sweet cane with money, neither hast thou filled me with the fat of thy sacrifices: but thou hast made me to serve with thy sins, thou hast wearied me with thine iniquities. ISAIAH 43:23, 24

The three great prophets of Israel allude to the sweet cane as a delicacy highly prized by the Jews. Jeremiah in his day inquires, *"To what purpose cometh there . . . sweet cane from a far country?"* JEREMIAH 6:20. Ezekiel also includes the sweet cane among the merchandise of the Phoenician traders. This cane is a stout perennial, is coarse, and grows to a height of fifteen feet; in mass it resembles a field of tall Indian corn. It is raised from shoots three inches in length, with leaves sprouting a few days after planting. These leaves are clear green and bamboolike in shape. Its little flowers are a soft honey-yellow and make a feathered spray, while the stems, green when young and maize-colored when ripe or dry, are solid and jointed. Sixteen months after planting, the cane is cut close to the ground. Its Latin name *Saccharum* is derived from the Greek word for sugar, *sakcharon*, and in Arabic it is called *souker*. Botanists have been unable to establish its native land, though its origin goes far back into history. China has known it for many centuries, and it is certainly a plant of the Old World. The plant was found in India and Arabia, and was carried by Arabs to North Africa and thence to the Mediterranean countries and the Holy Land.

Sweet Cane (sugar cane) Saccharum officinarum   Hebrew: kaneh
Thou hast bought me no sweet cane with money . . . ISAIAH 43:24

Sycamine
(black mulberry)

And the apostles said unto the Lord, Increase our faith. And the Lord said, If ye had faith as a grain of mustard seed, ye might say unto this sycamine tree, Be thou plucked up by the root, and be thou planted in the sea; and it should obey you.

LUKE 17:5, 6

Natives of the Grecian archipelago know the sycamine as *sycamenea;* it is actually the black mulberry. An ancient writer has recorded: "The sycamine is of no small height, very like the mulberie-tree in bigness and also like unto it in its leafe,—it groweth in Rhodes, and sundry places of Egypt." The large and oblong fruit looks like a blackberry. Its unusual construction is due to many separate blossoms gone to fruit and crowded closer together than a bunch of grapes. Heart-shaped leaves are slightly rough and of a rich green. The Chinese planted orchards of *Morus alba* to supply leaves for food for silkworms. Sycamine is referred to in the Apocrypha, where there is described a mighty battle in which elephants were used and sent into action. "*And to the end they might provoke the elephants to fight, they shewed them the blood of grapes and mulberries.*" I MACCABEES 6:34.

Sycamine (black mulberry) Morus nigra   Hebrew: shikmah

. . . ye might say unto this sycamine tree . . . LUKE 17:6

Sycomore

---

*Then answered Amos, and said to Amaziah, I
was no prophet, neither was I a prophet's son;
but I was an herdman, and a gatherer of sycomore fruit: and the Lord took me as I followed
the flock, and the Lord said unto me, Go, proph-
esy unto my people Israel.*   AMOS 7:14, 15

This quotation refers to an event which occurred while Amos
tended sheep and watched over the important orchards where
sycomore fig trees were planted. This sycomore is a curious tree
that combines the characteristics of both the fig and the mulberry; hence it is known as the mulberry-fig. The Arabs call it
glomez. Its height is that of an elm, and it bears its fruit directly
on the trunk and boughs. The yellowish fruit has black spots,
smells like an ordinary fig, but is inferior in taste. The green
leaves are firm and heart-shaped, resembling those of the mulberry. A large trunk parts into five or six stout branches not far
from the ground and, once planted, usually stands firm. Its porous
though very enduring wood was used for temples and audito-
riums, as well as for fashioning mummy chests or coffins, found in
perfect condition after more than three thousand years. The
New Testament mentions the sycomore in these words: *"And
Jesus entered and passed through Jericho. And, behold, there was
a man named Zacchaeus, which was the chief among the publi-
cans, and he was rich. And he sought to see Jesus who he was;
and could not for the press, because he was little of stature. And
he ran before, and climbed up into a sycomore tree to see him: for
he was to pass that way."* LUKE 19:1, 2, 3, 4.

(188)

Sycomore Ficus sycomorus   Hebrew: shikmoth

He destroyed their vines with hail, and their sycomore trees with frost.

PSALMS 78:47

Tares (darnel)

. . . The kingdom of heaven is likened unto a man which sowed good seed in his field: but while men slept, his enemy came and sowed tares among the wheat, and went his way. But when the blade was sprung up, and brought forth fruit, then appeared the tares also. So the servants of the householder came and said unto him, Sir, didst not thou sow good seed in thy field? from whence then hath it tares? He said unto them, An enemy hath done this. The servants said unto him, Wilt thou then that we go and gather them up? But he said, Nay; lest while ye gather up the tares, ye root up also the wheat with them.

MATTHEW 13:24, 25, 26, 27, 28, 29

The plant mentioned in this parable is the bearded darnel or rye grass, and resembles wheat so closely that it can prosper in the cornfields and be almost indistinguishable until fully grown. It flourishes in quantities in countries along the Mediterranean Sea. To the farmer it is one of the most destructive of all weeds, and in Eastern countries women and children are employed to pick out these tares before they ruin the good crop. As soon as the ears are formed, it is possible to recognize them, but both the wheat and the tares are usually left intermixed until after reaping. Then they are separated by a fanning that blows away the lighter and smaller seeds of the tares, and, after threshing, all seeds are shaken in a sieve. Thus any darnel seeds still remaining will usually pass through and leave the larger wheat behind. The inner coats of these seeds often harbor seriously poisonous fungus growths that, if eaten by humans or animals, will cause dizziness and vomiting and sometimes even death. Vergil calls it the *infelix lolium*, and the Arabs *siwan*.

Tares (darnel) Lolium temelentum   Greek: zizanion

. . . his enemy came and sowed tares among the wheat . . .

MATTHEW 13:25

The above illustration shows both wheat and tares. The tares are on the right.

Thistles

---

*And unto Adam he said, Because thou hast
hearkened unto the voice of thy wife, and hast
eaten of the tree, of which I commanded thee,
saying, Thou shalt not eat of it: cursed is the
ground for thy sake; in sorrow shalt thou eat
of it all the days of thy life; thorns also and
thistles shall it bring forth to thee; and thou shalt
eat the herb of the field.* GENESIS 3:17, 18

Successful plants in the hot and rocky regions of Israel grow
spines and thorns. The *Silybum* thistle is one of these. It is a tall
weed, lovely to look at, with flowers of clear mauve and leaves of
mottled silvery-green. Milk-white veins on the leaf surface also
give it the name "Mary's thistle." The star thistle, or *Centaurea
calcitrapa*, has golden yellow blossoms and thrives in every region
of Israel. In some places it grows over a foot high and makes
walking difficult. Thistle seeds have feathery growths attached to
them, which, when released, may float on the wind and land very
far away. When the rains come, another and still larger crop of
thistles begins its rapid growth in further distant areas.

Thistles Silybum marianum   Hebrew: dardar
          Centaurea calcitrapa

. . . *the thorn and the thistle shall come up to their altars* . . .

HOSEA 10:8

Crown of Thorns

And so Pilate, willing to content the people, released Barabbas unto them, and delivered Jesus, when he had scourged him, to be crucified. . . . And they clothed him with purple, and platted a crown of thorns, and put it about his head, and began to salute him, Hail, King of the Jews! MARK 15:15, 17, 18

This thorn plant, known as the Christ or Jerusalem thorn, is common throughout the Holy Land. It is accepted by many authorities as the shrub gathered by the soldiers to weave into the cruel crown they placed on Jesus' head. Other scholars favor the *Ziziphus spina-christi* as the thorn that was platted. The leaves of the *Paliurus* are green, oval-shaped and pointed, with incised veins running from the stalk to the tip. Tiny white flowers appearing in the spring later turn into dry, winged capsules that ripen between December and January. The shrub grows from three to nine feet in height, and its thorns, long, sharp, and recurved, often cause festering wounds.

Crown of Thorns Paliurus spina-christi   Greek: akantha
*And when they had platted a crown of thorns, they put it upon
his head . . .*   MATTHEW 27:29

Thorns

Beware of false prophets, which come to you in sheep's clothing, but inwardly they are ravening wolves. Ye shall know them by their fruits. Do men gather grapes of thorns, or figs of thistles? Even so every good tree bringeth forth good fruit; but a corrupt tree bringeth forth evil fruit. . . . Wherefore by their fruits ye shall know them. MATTHEW 7: 15, 16, 17, 20

Whole thickets of this spiny shrub cover large areas in all the warmer parts of Israel, especially the Jordan valley. Its branches grow in weird shapes, and are very tough and flexible. The thorns are sharp and the oval leaves are very bright green, with pointed tips and serrated edges. White flowers later develop into shiny orange berries the size of small plums. Planted as a hedge, this thorn is highly successful, for it forms an almost impenetrable fence. Arabs use it to keep goats and cattle off the fields. If, however, it is grown with crops, cattle will eat it as herbage. A liquor is also obtained from it. To the Arabs this thorn is known as *nubb*, and in parts of Israel is referred to as the "dhour tree."

Thorns Ziziphus spina-christi   Greek: akantha
Do men gather grapes of thorns, or figs of thistles? MATTHEW 7:16

Thorns (buckthorn)

And it shall come to pass in that day, that every place shall be, where there were a thousand vines at a thousand silverlings, it shall even be for briers and thorns. With arrows and with bows shall men come thither; because all the land shall become briers and thorns.   ISAIAH 7:23, 24

There are many varieties of thorns recorded in the Bible; this one is the Palestine buckthorn. It is an evergreen shrub or small tree, no taller than six feet in height, growing in thickets on the hillsides from Israel to Mount Sinai. In the southern section it is known as *sunwayd,* and in the northern part as *ajrayor.* The name *Rhamnus* is related to the Celtic word "*ram,*" meaning "branching." During March and April tiny flowerets appear on the stems. It has been used for centuries for planting hedges: "*Therefore, behold, I will hedge up thy way with thorns. . . .*" HOSEA 2:6. The stems were used as kindling, and thrown under the iron vessels in which meat was cooked. "*Before your pots can feel the thorns, he shall take them away as with a whirlwind, both living, and in his wrath.*" PSALMS 58:9. In old France a related species of buckthorn known as *reims* gave the city of Rheims its name. Today the city's coat of arms portrays two branches of intertwined buckthorn.

Thorns (buckthorn) Rhamnus palestina   Hebrew: chadek
The way of the slothful man is as an hedge of thorns: but the way
of the righteous is made plain.   PROVERBS 15:19

Thyine Wood

The merchandise of gold, and silver, and precious stones, and of pearls, and fine linen, and purple, and silk, and scarlet, and all thyine wood, and all manner vessels of ivory, and all manner vessels of most precious wood, and of brass, and iron, and marble, . . . And the fruits that thy soul lusted after are departed from thee, and all things which were dainty and goodly are departed from thee, and thou shalt find them no more at all. The merchants of these things, which were made rich by her, shall stand afar off for the fear of her torment, weeping and wailing, . . . For in one hour so great riches is come to nought. . . .

REVELATION 18:12, 14, 15, 17

This graphic account of the fall of the Antichrist's kingdom enumerates thyine wood among its costly merchandise. It was mentioned only this once in the Bible. The tree is small, slow-growing, and native to the Atlas Mountains in northwest Africa. It belongs to the cypress family, and is related to the arbor-vitae found in gardens. As a commodity the wood of the thyine or arar tree is almost priceless. It was used to burn as incense, and in the luxurious days of the Roman Empire this "citronwood" was highly prized in making ornamental woodwork. The timber is reddish-brown, very heavy and close-grained, and almost indestructible. Occasional knots in the lumber add to its value. In the ninth century thyine wood was used to build the celebrated mosque of Córdoba, now a cathedral. A whitish-yellow resin, virtually free from impurities and known commercially as sanderach, is obtained to use in the preparation of parchment. When the resin is dissolved in wine, it makes a delicate varnish.

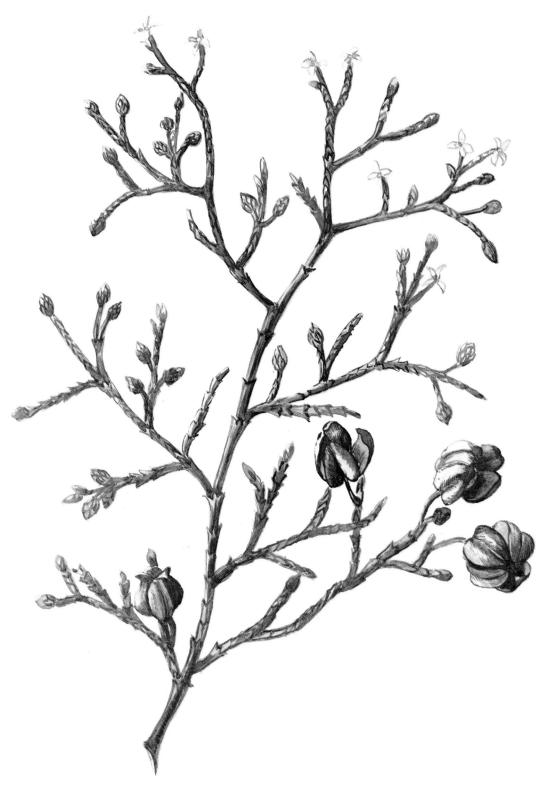

Thyine wood Tetraclinis articulata   Hebrew: etz avot

. . . and all thyine wood, and all manner vessels of ivory . . .

REVELATION 18:12

Vine (grape)

And he shall judge among many people, and rebuke strong nations afar off; and they shall beat their swords into plowshares, and their spears into pruninghooks: nation shall not lift up a sword against nation, neither shall they learn war any more. But they shall sit every man under his vine and under his fig tree; and none shall make them afraid: for the mouth of the Lord of hosts hath spoken it. MICAH 4:3, 4

The vine was cultivated before the flood, so that when Noah left the ark and stepped onto dry ground, he was able to plant a vineyard. This type of agriculture became one of the most important occupations in the Mediterranean world. The vine could be trained over a trellis, or supported by poles, though in most cases it was allowed to trail over the ground at will, or even climb to the tops of trees. Hillside plantings were best, and a watchman would guard the valuable vines from a booth or summer house. The grape harvest began by cutting the bunches with a sickle in July, and continuing through October. These bunches of grapes were thrown into a wine press, which was sometimes as large as a room and constructed underground, then trodden under foot by laborers. The juice of the squeezed grapes was made into wine and vinegar. This vinegar was poor or sour wine, chiefly the drink of the Roman soldiers. Egyptian grapes were small, so that one can realize the astonishment of the Israelites at their first view of the enormous clusters that the spies brought back from Eschol to Moses' camp (NUMBERS 13:23–26). The vine was honored most highly among the plants of the world when Jesus at his last supper declared: *"I am the true vine, and my Father is the husbandman."* JOHN 15:1.

(202)

Vine (grape) Vitis vinifera Hebrew: gephen
  And in the vine were three branches: and it was as though it budded,
  and her blossoms shot forth; and the clusters thereof brought forth
  ripe grapes . . . GENESIS 40:10

Vine of Sodom

*For their vine is of the vine of Sodom, and of the
fields of Gomorrah: their grapes are grapes of
gall, their clusters are bitter: . . . For the Lord
shall judge his people, and repent himself for his
servants, when he seeth that their power is gone,
and there is none shut up, or left.*

DEUTERONOMY 32:32, 36

One of the many thorny plants of the Holy Land is the apple of
Sodom. It bears only bitter fruit that looks like a tomato with its
flame-red skin, but it is not edible for it is full of hard black seeds
mingled with silky hairs resembling ashes. The Sodom apple, or
ampelos sodomorum, was known to the Greeks, and the Latin
peoples have many recorded references to the *kinea sodomorum*.
Josephus writes the story of a land which for its wickedness was
destroyed by fire, and where the presence of this fruit gave evidence of corruption. The shrub on which it grows reaches four
feet in height; its widely spreading branches, thickly covered
with short, sharp thorns, sprawl out on every side. The leaves are
long, with undulating edges, and its flowers resemble potato blossoms. This plant covers large areas around the Dead Sea and is
known as "dead sea fruit" or "dust and ashes."

Vine of Sodom Solanum sodomeum   Hebrew: gephen sêdom
. . . their vine is of the vine of Sodom . . . DEUTERONOMY 32:32

Water Lily

And the chapiters that were upon the top of the
pillars were of lily work in the porch, four
cubits. . . . And upon the top of the pillars was
lily work: so was the work of the pillars finished.
And he made a molten sea, ten cubits from the
one brim to the other. . . . And it was an hand
breadth thick, and the brim thereof was wrought
like the brim of a cup, with flowers of lilies. . . .

I KINGS 7:19, 22, 23, 26

Hiram of Tyre directed the interior decoration and the manufacture of the utensils of Solomon's Temple. The lily mentioned here is the one that floats on the surfaces of lakes and pools in Israel. It is a rich powder blue, with anthers of clear yellow. Fleshy stems grow up from a root not far below the bottom of the pool, and leaves that lie horizontally on the water help to support the flower. The scent of the flowers is odd and heavy. Because of its beauty, the plant is a great favorite in the gardens of the wealthy. The rootstocks contain an abundance of nutritious starchy mucilage and sugary matter, while the seeds are filled with floury albumen and are edible. In Nubia the natives use the seeds as a grain to make bread, and in Egypt the people eat both seeds and rootstocks.

Water Lily Nymphaea caerulea   Hebrew: shushan
And the chapiters that were upon the top of the pillars were of
lily work in the porch . . .   I KINGS 7:19

Wheat

---

*And it came to pass at the end of two full years,
that Pharaoh dreamed: and, behold, he stood by
the river. . . . And he slept and dreamed the
second time: and, behold, seven ears of corn
came up upon one stalk, rank and good. And,
behold, seven thin ears and blasted with the
east wind sprung up after them. And the seven
thin ears devoured the seven rank and full ears.
And Pharaoh awoke, and, behold, it was a dream.*

GENESIS 41:1, 5, 6, 7

The biblical term "corn" is synonymous with grain; it does not
refer to Indian maize, but usually to wheat, the most common cereal. Therefore Joseph, when asked to interpret Pharaoh's dream,
wisely counseled that all available harvests be stored in order to
meet the famine that was to come. Wheat is the most universally
used of all grains, and is sown in almost every part of the earth. Its
origin is so remote in time that the record of its beginning is lost.
Wheat brings a generous return for the care given it. This wheat
is a bearded variety that bears seven ears on one stalk, as in the
days of Joseph and the Pharaoh. The harvesting is done in June
by cutting the wheat down with sharp sickles. It is winnowed by
tossing it into the air against the wind to separate the grain from
the chaff, then it is sieved into large heaps. In Bible times a watchman always slept beside his mounds of winnowed wheat to protect them from thieves.

Wheat Triticum compositum   Hebrew: chittah

. . . and, behold, seven ears came up in one stalk, full and good . . .

GENESIS 41:22

The above illustration shows both wheat and tares. The wheat is on the left.

Wild Gourd

And Elisha came again to Gilgal: and there was a dearth in the land; and the sons of the prophets were sitting before him: and he said unto his servant, Set on the great pot, and seethe pottage for the sons of the prophets. And one went out into the field to gather herbs, and found a wild vine, and gathered thereof wild gourds his lap full, and came and shred them into the pot of pottage: for they knew them not. . . . they cried out, and said, O thou man of God, there is death in the pot. And they could not eat thereof.

II KINGS 4:38, 39, 40

Elisha, however, explained to the sons of the prophets that meal may be placed in the pot to counteract the bitterness of this wild gourd: "and there was no harm in the pot." The Hebrew word for this vegetable, when translated, means "to burst," and refers to its habit of breaking open when ripe. The plant, which resembles a cucumber, has a well-cut palmate and vinelike leaf that grows on a running stem along the ground. Its fruit is firm and round, varying in color from clear yellow to vivid orange, with green markings. When the fruit is ripe its pulp dries to form a powder used as a bitter medicine and drastic purgative. This powder is so inflammable that the Arabs collect it to use as kindling. In I KINGS 7:24 there is a description of a basin in the Temple of Solomon, on which this colocynth, carved in cedar wood, was used as ornamentation: "*And under the brim of it round about there were knops compassing it. . . .*" The gourd is known also as the "globe cucumber," and as "prophet's cucumber" from its biblical connotation.

Wild Gourd Citrullus colocynthis   Hebrew: pakknoth-sadeh
   . . . *and found a wild vine, and gathered thereof wild gourds his lap*
full . . .   II KINGS 4:39

Willow (aspen)

*By the rivers of Babylon, there we sat down,
yea, we wept, when we remembered Zion. We
hanged our harps upon the willows in the midst
thereof. For there they that carried us away captive required of us a song. . . . How shall we
sing the Lord's song in a strange land? If I
forget thee, O Jerusalem, let my right hand
forget her cunning.* PSALMS 137: 1, 2, 3, 4, 5

The willows of this text are thought to have been Euphrates
aspen trees that inhabit the banks of shallow rivers from Syria to
Israel, Arabia Petraea, and especially the Jordan valley. The tree
grows as high as forty-five feet. Its crisp leaves are borne on flat-
tened stems and attached obliquely to the main stalk. This causes
them to droop and hang down and continually sway back and
forth, like "weeping and wailing women." These leaves are only
one and a half inches long and heart-shaped; in the early spring
little green catkins appear among them. According to one legend,
this aspen furnished the wood for Jesus' cross, so that, ever since,
the leaves of all aspen trees have quivered and trembled.

Willow (aspen) Populus euphratica   Hebrew: 'arabim
We hanged our harps upon the willows . . . PSALMS 137:2

Willow

---

*Yet now hear, O Jacob my servant; and Israel,
whom I have chosen: . . . I will pour water
upon him that is thirsty, and floods upon the dry
ground: I will pour my spirit upon thy seed, and
my blessing upon thine offspring: And they shall
spring up as among the grass, as willows by the
water courses.* ISAIAH 44: 1, 3, 4

Biblical references to the willow are numerous. It is a common tree, growing in almost all climates and every country. Many species are found in the New World, as well as in Palestine. It favors moist places, and, as in the words of the Isaiah text, thrives best on the margins of rivers and brooks. The tree grows very rapidly and is easily propagated by cutting off slivers or slips, which, when pushed into moist earth, take root almost at once and spring up quickly. Thus Isaiah compares the willows by the water courses with those godly people who make quick progress in attaining spiritual wisdom. The roots bind the river bank and serve to keep it from being washed away by the flooding of the water. This tree has a beautiful long and narrow leaf: its upper surface is a clear rich green, and the underside is white. The leaves hang downward, as do the catkins which are its flowers. Salicene, a bitter principle extracted from the bark of young willow shoots, makes a good substitute for quinine. Willow branches were used by the Jews in some of their religious rites and ceremonies.

Willow Salix alba   Hebrew: 'arabim
  And they shall spring up as among the grass, as willows by the water
  courses.   ISAIAH 44:4

Wormwood

---

*And the third angel sounded, and there fell a
great star from heaven, burning as it were a lamp,
and it fell upon the third part of the rivers, and
upon the fountains of waters; And the name of
the star is called Wormwood: and the third part
of the waters became wormwood; and many men
died of the waters, because they were made bitter.* REVELATION 8:10, 11

The wormwood is frequently mentioned in Scripture, always for
its bitterness. *"Lest there should be among you man, or woman,
or family, or tribe, whose heart turneth away this day from the
Lord our God, to go and serve the gods of these nations; lest
there should be among you a root that beareth gall and wormwood."* DEUTERONOMY 29:18. This bitter juice is produced from
Artemisia, a genus named after the Greek goddess Artemis, and
known for centuries. One variety was called "parthenia" or "vir-
gin plant." Although there are many species in the genus, they all
look very much alike. The common wormwood of England has
been called mugwort since early times. It can grow to the size of a
small shrub and will send its side shoots right up the parent stem.
These shoots are covered with small green leaves that have a
woolly surface and light gray undersides. The leaves have a very
bitter taste and are used medicinally. The greenish-yellow flower
heads are small, round, and buttonlike. Oil of wormwood is a
source of absinthe.

Wormwood Artemisia judaica   Hebrew: laanah
Behold, I will feed them with wormwood, and make them drink the
water of gall . . .   JEREMIAH 23:15

Supplement I

Different Christian traditions give varying degrees of authority to the apocryphal books. In general, the Protestant community does not accept these books as part of the Scriptures. However, there are several plants mentioned in them that, if discussed, will give a more complete view of the Holy Land during Bible times. The first supplement shows these "apocryphal plants."

Aspalathus

*I gave a sweet smell like cinnamon and aspala-
thus, and I yielded a pleasant odour like the best
myrrh. . . . I am the mother of fair love, and
fear, and knowledge, and holy hope. . . .*

ECCLESIASTICUS 24:15, 18

These were the words of Jesus, son of Sirach, in praise of wisdom. All wisdom came from the Lord and was with Him forever,
and was likened to the plants that give the sweetest perfumes.
The aspalathus is one of these. A woody shrub with many small,
sharp thorns, it grows nearly shoulder high, bearing flowers that
give out a lovely perfume. The shrub yields the substance lignum
rhodianum, an essence of great fragrance much used by the ancients. Pliny describes the "aromatic aspalathus." Creamy white
blossoms are shaped like a morning glory, and are sometimes
flushed with pale pink. Fine-cut leaves are neatly arranged up the
stem. The Syrians call the plant deaxylon. It was used in prepar-
ing an ointment to thicken the hair and beards of the men, and as
a body perfume. A purgative drug is extracted by laying bare a
portion of the root and incising its outer covering. Each day
shells can be used to collect the juice from this root, which is a
lengthy one, about two feet long. Today the aspalathus grows
well along the shores of North Africa, and is found in the Canary
Islands.

.

Aspalathus Convolvulus floridus   Greek: aspalathos
I gave a sweet smell like cinnamon and aspalathus . . .
ECCLESIASTICUS 24:15

Ivy

Neither was it lawful for a man to keep sabbath days or ancient feasts, or to profess himself at all to be a Jew. And in the day of the king's birth every month they were brought by bitter constraint to eat of the sacrifices; and when the feast of Bacchus was kept, the Jews were compelled to go in procession to Bacchus, carrying ivy.

II MACCABEES 6:6, 7

Hedera is the Latin name of the ivy mentioned in this reading from the Apocrypha. A plant other than the European variety is indicated, for although its growth is similar, the fruit is gold rather than the usual purple-black. It is known as the Poet's variety. The flowers are creamy green, blooming in late autumn and remaining in blossom until February, when the berries form. Ivy is an evergreen climber with rich glossy green leaves. People in ancient times valued ivy highly, it being gathered and woven into chaplets to be worn at times of rejoicing. At heathen festivals the image of Bacchus, the god of wind, was usually crowned with ivy. This custom was believed to assure that no intoxication would attend the carnival.

Ivy Hedera helix
. . . *in procession to Bacchus, carrying ivy.* II MACCABEES 6:7

Lilies

---

*He was . . . as the flower of roses in the spring
of the year, as lilies by the rivers of waters, and
as the branches of the frankincense tree in the
time of summer.*   ECCLESIASTICUS 50:6, 8

Jesus, son of Sirach, was the poet who wrote these words about
Simon, the high priest, recorded in the Jewish-Greek literature of
Alexandria. This lily "by the rivers of waters" is known today as
an iris. It grows only twelve inches high, with strange straplike
leaves hugging the stalk from root to flower. This erect plant
keeps its place through tides and floods by forcing its tenacious
roots deep into the river banks. Most iris roots bear a delicate
odor. In the autumn they were lifted and dried in the shade,
many of them to be placed into linen chests to add perfume. The
women also threaded small pieces on long linen yarns to be hung
among garments in the household. When steeped in wine, the iris
or lily roots made a medicine believed to be efficacious in many
illnesses. The Palestine iris is very delicate in color, of soft lemon
and slight orchid-blue shade. "Iris" comes from the Greek word
for rainbow.

Lilies Iris palaestina   Hebrew: shushan
. . . *as lilies by the rivers of waters* . . . ECCLESIASTICUS 50:8

Manna

*And they said, Behold, we have sent you money
to buy you burnt offerings, and sin offerings,
and incense, and prepare ye manna, and offer
upon the altar of the Lord our God.*

BARUCH 1:10

Unusual plants are often mentioned in the Apocrypha. The shrub
camel's thorn is a low scrubby bush growing to a height of thirty-
six inches. It has spiny, hairy twigs, little creamy yellow, pea-like
blossoms, and very small leaves. Its family is Leguminosae or
Fabaceae. Throughout the day a sweet gummy substance may
exude from its many leaves and stems; this hardens when the cool
night air falls. In the early morning the sticky, yellow-white resin
is shaken from the stalks. A bush must be ten years old before the
gum will loosen. "Manna," "manna hebraica," and "Sinai manna"
are names by which this gum is known. It is not to be confused
with the manna sent from heaven to feed the children of Israel in
the wilderness. The allowance distributed to the Hebrews was
one omer a day, equal to two and a quarter pints in measure, and
two pounds in weight. Often, when a small insect punctures the
stem of the plant, the sugary liquid oozes out to harden into drops
collected and gathered into baskets by the Arabs. This manna is
found everywhere in the Sinai country, and is very common in
Palestine.

Manna Alhagi camelorum   Hebrew: mân

. . . *and prepare ye manna, and offer upon the altar* . . . BARUCH 1:10

Mastic Tree

Then said Daniel unto them, . . . Now then, if thou hast seen her, tell me, Under what tree sawest thou them companying together? Who answered, Under a mastick tree. SUSANNA 51, 54

This story appears in the Greek and Latin and first King James versions of the book of Daniel, but since it is not a part of the Hebrew Bible, it is not included in the final King James Version. The mastic or lentisc tree is an evergreen of medium size. There are, as a rule, eight leaflets on a stalk. These contain resin, and if ignited they will burn as fiercely as dry wood. Its branches are thick and crooked. The fruit resembles a hawthorn berry, and ripens to a reddish-brown that deepens to black. When they burn, both the fruit and the wood of the trunk give out a very pleasant aroma. This tree is common all along the Mediterranean coast, in the Holy Land, and in the Greek islands. Women living in harems use the resin obtained from the bark by incision. They chew it to sweeten their breath; hence this mastication gives the tree its name. Oil pressed from the berries is used by the Arabs for food and illumination. The twigs are light and flexible enough to be woven into baskets. In Algeria the tree forms dense copses along the coast. It is a very important Mediterranean shrub and yields annually, on the island of Scio alone, twenty-five thousand pounds of resin.

Mastic Tree Pistacia lentiscus   Hebrew: tzrai
Who answered, Under a mastick tree. SUSANNA 51, 54

Rose (oleander)

*Hearken unto me, ye holy children, and bud
forth as a rose growing by the brook of the
field: . . . bless the Lord in all his works. Mag-
nify his name, and shew forth his praise with the
songs of your lips, and with harps. . . .*
ECCLESIASTICUS 39: 13, 14, 15

According to careful students of the Scriptures, the oleander is
the "rose of the waterbrooks"—the "rhododendron" or "rose
tree" of the Greeks. A tall flowering shrub is indicated by the
context; the oleander is such a plant, as it grows to twenty feet in
height. A traveler through Israel finds it one of the most beautiful
shrubs of that country; it flourishes in warm locations, and grows
abundantly near streams or alongside wells—any place where
there is water. In the spring it shows masses of bloom, though
they may vary from white to red, or even to purple. To the
Spanish it is known as "laurel," and is their favorite shrub for
parks and gardens. As a member of the dogbane family this
flower, and even the whole shrub, is highly poisonous, and must
be handled with care. As an evergreen summer favorite, it is
termed "tough and attractive," and does well in almost any soil.
The blooms last all through the summer months. It was revered
by the early Christians as the flower of St. Joseph.

Rose (oleander) Nerium oleander

. . . *and bud forth as a rose growing by the brook* . . .

ECCLESIASTICUS 39:13

Rose

Thus saith the Lord unto Esdras, Tell my people that I will give them the kingdom of Jerusalem, which I would have given unto Israel. For thy help will I send my servants Esay and Jeremy, after whose counsel I have sanctified and prepared for thee twelve trees laden with divers fruits, And as many fountains flowing with milk and honey, and seven mighty mountains, whereupon there grow roses and lilies, whereby I will fill thy children with joy. II ESDRAS 2:10, 18, 19

This Phoenician rose is a large bush rose, growing from three to nine feet tall. From its base spread out long branches covered with hooked thorns. The leaflets grow in pairs on their rachis, with one at the apex or tip. They are yellow-green, with a shiny surface and serrate edges. This is a cluster rose with a sweet perfume, and it is fairly free from the attacks of insects. The flowers are white and shaped like the wild rose of the west, with bright centers filled with golden stamens. So numerous are the blossoms that as many as forty can bloom on one branch. After the petals drop, the usual form of rose hip, or fruit, appears, coloring red as it develops. As the text indicates, this rose likes altitude; it inhabits the mighty mountains in Israel, even at an elevation of six thousand feet. Gardeners like this rose, which responds so favorably to care and training over an arbor.

Rose Rosa phoenicia
. . . *mighty mountains, whereupon there grow roses and lilies* . . .
II ESDRAS 2:19

Turpentine Tree
(teil tree)

As the turpentine tree I stretched out my branches, and my branches are the branches of honour and grace. ECCLESIASTICUS 24:16

The Hebrew word, translated literally, means "strong," so undoubtedly it refers to a sturdy tree. It is not the evergreen oak, for that is separately named in the passage ". . . *as a teil tree, and as an oak, whose substance is in them, when they cast their leaves. . . .*" ISAIAH 6:13. The teil is not a tall tree, but is of spreading habit, with a trunk and boughs of great thickness. The wood is hard and white. Its foliage is thick enough to cast a very dense shade on the deserts heated in the sun. This is thought to be the tree under which the angel of the Lord sat and spoke with Gideon: "*And there came an angel of the Lord, and sat under an oak which was in Ophrah, . . . and said unto him, The Lord is with thee, thou mighty man of valour.*" JUDGES 6:11, 12. The tree stands alone, and not in forests. Its leaves are a rich coppery green, and red berries hang in clusters like currants. When the bark is cut, turpentine flows out: this has an agreeable perfume, not unlike jessamine, and is mild to the taste. Exposure to the air solidifies it to a transparent gum. The turpentine tree is a Mediterranean tree, but does not reach fine proportions there as it does in Israel.

Turpentine Tree (teil tree) Pistacia trebinthus var. palaestina Hebrew: elah
. . . *as a teil tree, and as an oak, whose substance is in them, when they
cast their leaves . . .*   ISAIAH 6:13

Supplement II

The prints on previous pages show in form, and the descriptions depict in words, more than one hundred biblical plants. These supplementary notes will attempt to show the remaining few of "All the Plants of the Bible."

Bitter Herbs

Besides the illustrated dandelion, several different plants were in the regular diet and in use on special holy-day occasions, depending upon what ones were available in the various localities. They were chichory, *Cichorium endivia* and *C. intybus*, lettuce, *Latuca sativa*, watercress, *Nasturtium officinale*, sorrel, *Rumex acetosella* var. *multifidus*, and *Mint*, mentioned elsewhere.

Candlesticks

The seven-branched *Candlesticks* mentioned in EXODUS 37 probably took their form in man's hands from the pattern that nature provided in the inflorescence of the Judean sage, *Salvia judaica*.

Cereals

Other species of *Barley* besides the one illustrated were raised, better suited to the divergent growing conditions of the area and providing different times for maturing grain. These were the winter barley, *Hordeum hexastichon*, and the spring barley, *H. vulgare*. The *Rie* of Exodus and Isaiah and the *Fitches* of EZEKIEL 4 were spelt, *Triticum aestivum* var. *spelta*.

Flags

The *Flags*, other *Rushes* and *Meadows* of certain Old Testament passages were similarly growing plants now known as the flowering rush or water gladiole, *Butomus umbellatus*, the hard rushes which are species of *Juncus* and the clubrushes which are species of *Scirpus*.

Grasses and Straw

In Bible times the Holy Land must have had many kinds of *Grasses* growing over its assorted types of land, although probably not as many as at the present time because throughout the years travelers have intentionally and unintentionally brought in scores of new ones. Some of the more important ancient ones were *Aegilops variabilis, Alopecurus anthoxanthoides, Avena sterilis, Eragrostis megastachya, Nardurus orientalis*, and *Polypogon monspeliensis*, and are probably those referred to as grass in the Scriptures.

Heath

Jeremiah alluded to the *Heath* in the desert or wilderness. It was probably the brown-berried cedar, *Juniperus oxycedrus*.

Husks

The Prodigal Son "would fain have filled his belly with the husks that the swine did eat" according to LUKE 15:16. These husks were the pods of the carob tree, *Ceratonia siliqua*.

Many biblical commentators, studying MATTHEW 3:4, now believe that these "carob beans" or "locust pods" were used by John the Baptist in his honey and locust diet rather than actual insects.

Lilies

The *Lily* designs of the Temple were taken from such water lilies as the blue one mentioned in this book and also from the white one, *Nymphaea alba*, and the white Egyptian lotus, *N. lotus*. Besides the three Bible *Lilies* already illustrated here, there were at least two others—the recently verified madonna lily, *Lilium candidum*, and hyacinth among which the animals browsed in King Solomon's gardens, *Hyacinthus orientalis*.

Manna

The *Manna* that could be purchased was the gum resin not only *of Alhagi camelorum* illustrated but also that of such trees as *Tamarix mannifera* and probably *Fraxinus ornus*. The *Manna* for EXODUS 16 "which grew up in the night, when the ground was moist" and which melted "when the sun waxed hot" was some species of simple alga called *Nostoc*. The *Manna* of NUMBERS 11 that fell from the heavens at night probably consisted of several lowly lichens such as *Lecanora affinis*, *L. esculenta*, and *L. fruticulosa* from the vast barren mountains in western Asia and northern Africa.

Onycha

Another *Onycha*, the one in EXODUS 30, may have been derived from *Styrax benzoin*.

Reeds

The *Reeds* of MATTHEW 27 and MARK 15 were of two sorts. The one used for attaching the sponge (spunge) of vinegar was most probably what is now called dhura, *Sorghum vulgare* var. *durra*, while the one placed in Jesus' hand as a mock scepter and used to smite his head was in all probability the giant reedmace or cattail, *Typha angustata*.

Sope

The *Soap* and *Washing-balls* of the Bible were made from the burnt alkali ash of the saltworts, *Salsola inermis* and *S. kali*, and the jointed glassworts, *Salicornia fruticosa* and *S. herbacea*.

Sweet Cane (Calamus)

The biblical *Canes* were sweet in either taste or smell. The aromatic ones were mentioned in EXODUS 30:23–24, I KINGS 10:10, SONG OF SOLOMON 4:14, JEREMIAH 6:20, and EZEKIEL 27:19 under the terms *Calamus*, *Sweet Cane*, or *Spices*. They are now generally identified as the ginger grass, *Andropogon aromaticus*.

They could not have been the *Acorus calamus* because that plant originally came from North America and therefore was not known in Bible lands in Bible days. The truly saccharine ones were mentioned in JOSHUA 16:8, 19:28, and ISAIAH 43:24 under this term or the place name *Kanah* where they grew. They are now generally identified as the sugar cane, *Saccharum officinarum*. The plant was used directly for sweetening. It was not until the seventh century A.D. that sugar processing was used by the Jews.

Thorny Plants

Twenty-two different terms were used in the Hebrew versions of the Bible for the many, many armored plants of this area. The task of identifying them accurately has been extremely difficult. Only after much study have the following scientific guesses been offered beyond those already mentioned in this book:

the *Thistles* of JOB 31 as the Syrian thistle, *Notobasis syriaca*,
the *Brambles* of ISAIAH 34 as the spotted golden thistle, *Scolymus maculata* and *Rubus sanctus* elsewhere,
the *Thorns* of HOSEA 9 as the burweed, *Xanthium spinosum*,
several *Stinging Nettles* as assorted species of *Urtica*,
the *Nettles* of PROVERBS 24 as the charlock, *Sinapis arvensis*,
the *Briers* of MICAH 7 as the Palestine nightshade, *Solanum incanum*,
and the *Pricking Brier* of EZEKIEL 28 as the prickly butcher's-broom, *Ruscus aculeatus*.

Trees

Besides those already depicted in this book, the following are best identified as:

the *Thick Trees* of LEVITICUS 23 as the Brutian pine, *Pinus brutia*,
the *Elms* of HOSEA 4, the *Teil* tree of ISAIAH 6, and the *Turpentine Tree* of the twenty-fourth chapter of the apocryphal book ECCLESIASTICUS, all as the Palestine terebinth, *Pistacia terebinthus*,
other species of *Oaks* as *Quercus coccifera*, *Q. c.* var. *pseudococcifera*, and *Q. lusitanica* (and on some of these lived

the scale insect which was the source of the biblical *Scarlet*),

the *Trees in Ramah* of I SAMUEL 22, the *Trees in Jabesh* of
I SAMUEL 31, and the *Grove in Beersheba* of GENESIS 21,
all as tamarisks, *Tamarix articulata*, *T. pentandra*, and
T. tetragyna,

the *Shady Trees* of JOB 40 as the lotus bush, *Ziziphus lotus*,

the *Withs* of JUDGES 16 and other *Willows* of the Old Testament as *Salix acmophylla*, *S. fragilis*, and *S. safsaf*,

the *Cedar Wood* of LEVITICUS 14 as the Phoenician juniper,
Sabina phoenicia.

Weeds

The *Weeds* that became wrapped around Jonah's head were
likely the marine eelgrass, *Zostera marina*.

Note on Plant Terms

There are many plant terms used in the Scriptures that refer to
parts or structures, such as *Bud, Fruit, Stem, Leaf, Branch*, etc.
There are others that refer to groups or growths, such as *Stubble,
Forests*, etc. Sometimes the identification is obvious from the context; sometimes it can only be guessed at; sometimes it is only to
be taken figuratively in either a very general or in a specific way.

This book deals in general only with the flowering plants of the
Bible, and consequently no detailed attempt is made to discuss or
illustrate the algae, fungi, lichens, mosses, and ferns. The *Blue
Dye* from the lichen *Roccella tinctoria* is mentioned in several
places in the Old Testament. The work of the simple organisms
of *Vinegar, Wine*, and *Strong Drink* formation, the leavening
yeasts and the causal organisms responsible for *Ague, Fevers,
Boils, Scall, Issues of Blood* (that were associated with illnesses),
Plagues, Moldings, Blastings, Sores, Consumption, and *Leprosy*
might well be added to the lists of plants to make it more complete. Their exact identification may be learned in more detailed
texts in this field.